PATRIOTISM

THE NATIONS
BELIEVERS

JOHN GRAHAM

Table of content

Chapter 1. What is Patriotism?

For a definition, individuals with patriot leanings scorn the ascending of globalization in very much arranged plans and political establishments. There is a somewhat enormous supplement on putting public interests and needs before generally speaking ones, as such the name "positive energy." Patriotism supposedly is rotated around the 'social unit of the country.' In any case, for a fundamental piece of history, one's political leanings were not dependent upon public endpoints.

This changed in Europe after the Protestant Change. The state turned out to be more liable to individuals who withstood inside the nation rather than outside powers like the Catholic Church. A little while later, positive energy and certainty became indispensable pieces of the perspective on the larger part of controls government.

Patriotism is a serious strong region for the of a country, correspondingly as specific energy. Self-finishing up certain energy recommends a longing for a state spread out in a self-character. This is the explanation of white positive energy, the longing for a white state. Certain individuals could recognize that positive energy is spread out in the American story and that without it the Constitution in all probability won't exist. In any case, all things being equal, predisposition and extremist individuals by and large tended to and upheld by Donald Trump's sort of certain energy.

Once more the mission of "America First" and "Make America Extraordinary" is set in a particularly patriot bearing. The essential issue with this position is that Donald Trump's meaning of "American" prohibits various social events who live in the US. This is called ethnonationalism. A few events of the ethnonationalist philosophies utilized by Donald Trump and his party solidify the creation and interest with the breaking point wall between the US and Mexico, the Muslim boycott, and the strong detachment of families along the Mexican line, among different others. Fundamentally, an ascending in white positive energy has happened, invigorated by the Donald Trump base.

Ramifications of patriotism have wavered, similar to the relationship between "excitement" and such considerations as "positive energy" and "public affiliation" (Bonikowski 2016b). Sociologists zeroing in on the irrefutable early phases of country states traditionally conceptualize positive energy as a perspective that started

by political elites: "a political standard, which holds that the political and the public unit ought to be compatible" (Gellner 1983:1). Political analysts, who will generally concentrate on mentalities toward the country in laid out popular governments, comprehend patriotism all the more barely, frequently in wording firmly connected to specific review things. Some depict "patriotism" as "enthusiasm's" harmful malicious twin, characterizing the previous as "a view of the public prevalence and a direction toward public strength" and the last option as "a profoundly felt emotional connection to the country" (Kosterman and Feschbach 1989:271).

Others make comparative qualifications without referencing "patriotism" by any stretch of the imagination, rather alluding to "blind" and "productive" types of positive energy (Schatz, Staub, and Levine 1999).

Patriotism Throughout History

During the Modern Transformation, it became obvious that parts of a common personality, like shared proficiency in a solitary language, would mean quite a bit to a country's prosperity. In this manner, the digestion of gatherings beyond the aggregate standard of the nation became seen as a first concern.

This absorption occurred through municipal establishments yet additionally through ethnic purifying, war, and other vicious strategies to crash any societies or customs viewed as "various" from the country's own. During the 1900s, there was a detachment made between the thoughts of 'liberal private enterprise' and 'patriot a majority rules government.' This set of experiences illustration is to portray the back-and-forth movements of patriotism over the entire course of time. It is entirely expected to observe a resurgence of patriotism, but it is essential to comprehend the unfortunate results to explore the resurgence in the best manner for all gatherings.

J. S. Mills's meaning of patriotism:

A piece of humankind might be said to comprise an ethnicity on the off chance that they are joined among themselves by normal feelings which don't exist among them and any others — which make them co-work with one another more enthusiastically than with others, want to be under a similar government, and want that it ought to be government without help from anyone else, or a part of themselves, solely.

Mills then, at that point, records numerous collinear reasons for normal public opinion starting with, indeed, "the impact of personality of race and plummet." Factory proceeds to make light of nationality to some degree by contending that the "most grounded [source] of all [national sentiments] is the character of political predecessors." However, on the off chance that most countries were generally bound together by identity, nationalities will likewise have a typical history of political precursors

Americans are extraordinary in numerous ways, to a great extent since we have a fundamental liberal philosophy that is not at all like to the point that of different nations. All things being equal, American patriots are not extraordinary and are the same as their philosophical brethren abroad. A new Majority rules government Asset overview asked how significant legitimate, conduct and unchanging qualities are for being an American. Everyone concurred that citizenship and regard for American establishments made a difference — which we'd expect to find in a nation established on a liberal belief system. Notwithstanding, the most nationalistic gathering of Americans in the overview (called American

Preservationists) additionally believed that ethnic, locational, and social definitions were relatively vital for being an American.

As per the Majority rules government Asset overview of Trump allies, American Preservationists are 20 to 50 focuses more probable than different gatherings of Trump allies to say that it is "vital" to have specific ethnic and social identifiers to be genuinely American. Of those ethno- social attributes that they esteem, 69% say being brought into the world here, 67% say having lived in America for the vast majority of one's life, and 59 percent say being Christian. Most upsetting, 47% of them said that it is entirely or to some degree essential to be of European plummet to be genuinely American.

The Ancien System in France made present-day patriotism. It was spread through the French Transformation and Napoleonic Conflicts as an administration's misleading publicity instrument to bring down the expense of military preparation. It's less expensive for the public authority to persuade men to battle on the off chance that they accept they will battle for a country of which they are everlastingly a part as opposed to for a far-off government or ruler whom they don't by and by having the foggiest idea. That is the reason the state is fundamental to present-day patriotism: it's the central recipient, as public undertakings are quite often driven by the public authority.

Present-day patriotism depends on a central identity, however, it expands on that center through friendly design, consequently the expression "nation- building." French patriot Emmanuel Sieyes discussed the need to make "every one of the pieces of France a solitary body, and every one individual who partition it into a solitary body." At Sieyes' time, France was brimming with various nationalities that didn't consider themselves

French — the Bretons, Normans, and Basques. He proceeded to contend that "the country is preceding everything. It is the wellspring of everything."

Another French patriot, Henri Gregoire, said that residents must be "dissolved into the public mass." The dramatist Marie-Joseph Chenier composed that the objective of the post-Transformation schooling system was "to frame Frenchmen, to enrich the country with its own, extraordinary physiognomy" (accentuation added). Constrained absorption of the non-French ethnic gatherings into an already- existing French identity — addressed by the spread of the French language — was the objective of the French patriots. Until the late nineteenth or mid-twentieth hundred years, French was the principal language of a minority of residents.

There are three variations of present-day patriotism all over the place: an administration takes on the philosophy to legitimize an expansion an option for its; an untouchable gathering inside the state professes to address the "genuine country"; an outcast gathering professes to address a different country to construct its professes to power or withdrawal. In practically this large number of cases, the center of the country is an ethnic gathering that should be developed and extended to the detriment of other ethnic gatherings. For that reason patriotism can be an old philosophy that should be both made and sustained by the state, best summarized by the Italian patriot Massimo d'Azeglio who said, "Italy is made, however, who will currently make Italians?"

George Orwell composed that the "reason for each patriot is to get more power and more eminence, not so much for himself but rather for the country or other unit wherein he has decided to sink his singularity." He happened by expressing that patriotism is very unmistakable from positive energy, which is a "dedication to a specific spot and a specific lifestyle, which one accepts to be the most incredible on the planet, however, has no wish to compel on others. Positive energy is its inclination protective, both militarily and socially. Patriotism, then again, is indistinguishable from the longing for power." Patriotism is the soundness of the state.

Patriots in each nation have been the most strong of wars. It's one thing to embrace patriotism and cheerfully remark that "the right of others to self-government" is significant, however, various patriots differ over which countries appropriately own what parcels, whether co- ethnics in various nations ought to be essential for the nation-state addressing that ethnic gathering, and whether a few gatherings even comprise countries. At the point when countries differ over these things, they frequently battle wars — some legitimately.

Israeli patriots and Palestinian patriots differ about whether the other gathering is a country that has a genuine case for the challenged land in the Center East. The untrustworthy patriot's reaction is to guarantee that is not a genuine model since either country is not genuine. In any case, patriots in the two countries think their country is genuine, that its cases are predominant, and that they merit battling for. Whenever called upon, both would safeguard their country with viciousness. Patriots' case that their philosophy isn't strategic resembles socialists' refusal to concede that their philosophy would prompt the confiscation of private property.

The ongoing ascent of patriotism is an update that the two wings of the American political range are neighborly to dictatorship, whether it's socialism on the left or patriotism on the right.

Benefits and Dangers of Patriotism

Patriotism can be used for improvement. Over the entire course of time, patriotism can be credited to an ascent in the trading of homegrown items, enlistment in the military, and general positive energy. The possibility of a common personality associated with a nation is an inspiration among residents.

In Korea and Taiwan, authorities had the option to carry out the Japanese enlivened hierarchical patriot model that extraordinarily energized development. Be that as it may, patriotism can likewise energize prohibition and rivalry. In Europe, colonialism and colonization were frequently legitimate by patriotism. These were two strategies utilized by western nations to overwhelm and control nations in Africa and Asia, the very unfortunate results of which are as yet being seen today. During The Second Great War, Adolf Hitler utilized patriot strategies to get his base and legitimize his strategies for the well-being of Germany. Patriot feeling, seen as laying out one gathering to be the legitimate residents of a nation, is hazardous in an undeniably globalized world.

Chapter 2: Patriotism Across the Globe

After 2016, there was an enormous ascent in patriot opinion across the world. Maybe the most well-known stage for this peculiarity was the US with the appointment of Donald Trump, who ran on a patriot stage with the trademark, "America First." In Germany, the patriot AfD party has turned into significant resistance, and in Spain conservative Vox has become unmistakable inside the Spanish Parliament. Additionally, patriot pioneers have climbed onto the political stage in China, the Philippines, and Turkey.

Countries are not generally comprised of a solitary ethnic, strict, or language bunch. This expansion in exclusionary patriotism that we are seeing could end up being possibly exceptionally hazardous for the gatherings viewed as "untouchables." It is essential to comprehend a wide range of features of patriotism to safeguard against the unfortunate results it brings as these political pioneers ascend in prevalence.

In "The Situation for Patriotism," Rich Lowry characterizes patriotism as moving from a group's "regular dedication to their home and their country." Yoram Hazony, in his book "The Righteousness of Patriotism," likewise has a somewhat anesthetic meaning of patriotism. It signifies "that the world is administered best when countries consent to develop their practices, liberated from obstruction by different countries."

There isn't anything especially questionable by any stretch of the imagination about these proclamations. Characterized in these terms, it seems like minimal more than essentially safeguarding identity or public power, which is the reason Lowry, Hazony, and others demand their meaning of patriotism doesn't have anything to do with the most destructive structures including nationality, race, militarism, or one-party rule.

The issue lies here. We guess any of us can take any practice that has an unmistakable history and essentially reclassify it however we would prefer. We could then allow ourselves to reprimand any individual who disagrees with us as a "misconception" or in any event, criticize us.

Be that as it may, who is answerable for getting here wrong? Individuals who are attempting to reclassify the term, or individuals who help us to remember patriotism's genuine history and what patriotism has been ever? Which brings up a significantly greater issue: Why go down this street by any stretch of the imagination?

On the off chance that you need to invest half of your energy making sense of, "Gracious, we don't imply that sort of patriotism," how could you need to relate a respected practice of American municipal enthusiasm, public pride, and American transcendence by any stretch of the imagination with the different patriotisms that have happened on the planet? All things considered, American preservationists have contended that an extraordinary aspect concerning America was that it was unique from any remaining nations. Not quite the same as any remaining patriotisms.

Patriotism isn't the same thing as a public personality. It's not the same thing as regard for public power. It's not even the same thing as public pride. It's something by and large and insightfully unique, and those distinctions are not simply semantic, specialized, or the distractions of scholastic students of history. They go to the actual quintessence of being an American.

We assume we comprehend the reason why certain individuals will be drawn to the idea of patriotism. President Trump utilized the term patriotism. Public preservationists imagine that President Trump has taken advantage of another populism for traditionalism, and they need to exploit it. They believe that conventional fusionist traditionalism and the American transcendence thought are not sufficient. These thoughts are not sufficiently strong. They need something more grounded to confront the all-inclusive cases of globalism and reformism that they accept are hostile to America. They additionally need something more grounded to push back on open boundaries and boundless migration.

We figure out that. We see very well the craving to have a strong response to the impropriety of worldwide administration and globalism, and we have no difficulty at all contending that a worldwide framework in light of country states and public power is immeasurably predominant, particularly for the US, to one that is controlled by a worldwide overseeing body that is equitably remote from individuals.

So what's the issue then, at that point? For what reason can't we simply all concur that patriotism characterized in this manner is what we American preservationists have been and trusted from the beginning — that it's a new, more in-vogue bottle for an exceptionally old wine? Indeed, the new container significantly has an impact on the way that the wine will be seen. For what reason do we want another container by any stretch of the imagination? It would resemble placing a completely decent California cabernet in a container marked from Germany or France or Russia or China.

The issue lies in that little postfix, "ism." It demonstrates that the word patriotism implies a general practice, framework, reasoning, or philosophy that is valid for all. There is a practice of patriotism out there that we Americans are important for. All nations have "patriotism." All countries and all people groups are undeniably recognized for what makes them unique. Their normal legacy as patriots is their distinction. Their various dialects, their various nationalities, their various societies.

Simultaneously, all countries as far as anyone knows share similar power and privileges of the country state, no matter what their type of government. A sovereign popularity-based country state is, in this regard, the same as a sovereign dictator country state. No matter what the various types of government are, it's the shared characteristic of the country express that is important. Subsequently, the power of Iran or North Korea is, from this perspective, ethically and legitimately the same as the sway of the US or some other popularity-based country.

We immovably accept that not all country states are something very similar. There have been times in history when countries have been related to prejudice, ethnic matchless quality, militarism, socialism, and totalitarianism. Does that imply that all country states are like that? Not, however, there is a tremendous distinction between the verifiable peculiarities of patriotism and regard for the power of a popularity-based country state. Patriotism commends social and, surprisingly, ethnic contrasts of a group, no matter what the type of government. The popularity-based country state, then again, grounds its authenticity and its power inequitable administration.

The most concerning issue causing this misconception isn't perceiving the genuine history of patriotism. It is, as we referenced previously, to confound public personality, public cognizance, and public power with Patriotism with a capital N.

Patriotism as we generally realize it emerged not in America but rather in Europe. Our freedom development was a revolt of individuals over the sort of government that we had under the English. The originators at first considered themselves British blokes, who were being denied their privileges by Parliament and by the crown. Indeed, Americans unquestionably had a personality, however, it was not in light of nationality, language, or even religion alone. It had proactively fostered an exceptionally unmistakable comprehension of self-government, and that was the way to the Transformation.

At this point, Americans previously had a genuinely impressive feeling of personality, however, that character was not patriotism. Why would that be? Since patriotism had not been developed at this point. There was no such thing as it at the hour of the American Transformation.

Present-day patriotism started in France, during the French Transformation. The transformation was an invitation to the battle of the French public. The French country was brought into the world in the French Transformation. The dread and Napoleonic colonialism were the most noteworthy articulation of this new-conceived French patriotism.

Napoleon's patriot colonialism, thusly, ignited the ascent of counter-traditionalist patriotism in Germany, and all over Europe. Germans, Russians, Austrians, and different countries found their public cognizance and the significance of their societies in their contempt of the French trespassers.

From that point forward, patriotism seethed across the nineteenth and twentieth hundred years as a festival of countries in light of the normal public culture and a typical language, and a typical verifiable encounter. Patriotism was, in this sense, particularistic. It was populistic. It was restrictive. It was lost. It celebrated contrasts, not the normal humankind of Christianity as it had been known in the Heavenly Roman Domain or the Catholic Church or even in the Illumination.

The way to patriotism was the country state. It wasn't simply individuals who were free or sovereign as individuals, however, individuals were addressed by and for the sake of the country state. At the end of the day, their state-run administrations. Power eventually dwelled in the state, not individuals. The state was over individuals, not of, by, and for individuals as in the American experience. Right up to the present day, this thought lives in the English government, for instance, where the Sovereign is definitive, not individuals or the Parliament.

It is tragically a typical verifiable mistake to compare patriotism with the verifiable ascent of the country state in Europe and the worldwide state framework that emerged after the Tranquility of Westphalia in 1648. The Westphalian Harmony perceived the power of rulers, over and against the all-inclusive cases of the Heavenly Roman Domain and the Congregation, and the facts confirm that the Protestant Reorganization hardened the sway of the sovereigns and the territories as trailblazers to the country state.

Be that as it may, these were sovereigns. They were governments. They were administrations. It was only a lot later that the cutting-edge country state and particularly the well-known opinions of patriotism emerged ever. In any case, this state framework isn't patriotism. Patriotism is a memorable peculiarity that didn't arise for an additional 150 years after 1648. Guaranteeing in any case is terrible history, straightforward as can be.

That carries us to the possibility of American transcendence, which is, we accept, the response to the subject of America's public personality and what it ought to be.

A delightful idea catches both the truth and the equivocalness of the American experience. It depends on an all-inclusive statement of faith. It is grounded in America's establishing standards: regular regulation, freedom, restricted government, individual privileges, the balanced governance of government, well-known power not the sway of the folkish country express, the acculturating job of religion in common society, and not a laid out religion related with one class or one statement of faith, and the significant job of common society and common foundations in establishing and interceding our majority rules system and our opportunity.

We as Americans accept these standards are correct and valid for all people groups and not only for us. That was the way that

Washington and Jefferson figured out them, and it was unquestionably the way that Lincoln grasped them. That makes them all-inclusive. At the end of the day, the American statement of faith grounds us in widespread standards.

Be that as it may, what, you might ask, makes us so extraordinary then, at that point? On the off chance that it's all-inclusive, what makes us extraordinary? It is, as a matter of fact, the statement of faith.

We accept that Americans are different because our statement of faith is both widespread and extraordinary simultaneously. We are extraordinary in the one-of-a-kind way we apply our widespread standards. It doesn't be guaranteed to imply that we are superior to different people groups, however, I figure presumably most Americans in all actuality do accept that they are. It's not exactly about gloating privileges. Rather, it's undeniably true that there is something else extraordinary about the US, which gets derailed while talking with regards to patriotism.

A patriot can't say this, since there isn't anything all-inclusive about patriotism with the exception that all patriotisms are, indeed, unique and particularistic. Patriotism is without any trace of a typical thought or guideline of government except that a group or a country state can be nearly anything. It very well may be fundamentalist, it tends to be dictator, it very well may be authoritarian, or it very well may be popularity based.

A portion of the new patriots question unequivocally the significance of the American statement of faith. They contend that the statement of faith isn't generally so significant as we naturally suspected it was to our public personality. We should simply contemplate that briefly.

What's the significance here to say that the statement of faith truly isn't exactly significant? On the off chance that the statement of faith doesn't make any difference, why is America so extraordinary?

Is it our language? All things considered, no. We share that with England, and presently a significant part of the world.

Is it our nationality? Indeed, that doesn't work either because a typical American nationality can't possibly exist.

Is it a particular religion? We are without a doubt a strict nation, however, no, we have the opportunity of religion, not one explicit religion.

Is it our delightful waterways and mountains? No. We have a few delightful waterways and mountains, however, so do different nations.

Is it our way of life? Indeed, let's assume all in all, yet how would we figure out American culture without the American statement of faith and the establishing standards?

Lincoln referred to America as the world's "last best expectation," since it was where everything individuals can and ought to be free. Before Lincoln, Jefferson called it a domain of freedom.

Foreigners came here and turned out to be valid Americans by living the American statement of faith and the Pursuit of happiness. You can turn into a French resident, however for most Frenchmen, on the off chance that you are unfamiliar, that isn't the same thing as being French. It's different here. You can be a genuine American by embracing our statement of faith and our lifestyle.

After The Second Great War, the American way and our dedication to a majority rules government turned into a reference point of opportunity for the entire world. That was the underpinning of our case to world administration in the Virus War, and it is the same today. On the off chance that we become a country very much like some other country, then, at that point, honestly we wouldn't anticipate that some other country should concede us any extraordinary trust or backing.

One more advantage of American transcendence is that it is self-rectifying. At the point when we neglect to satisfy our standards as we did with subjugation before the Nationwide conflict, we can request as Lincoln did to our "better nature" to address our imperfections. That is where the focal significance of the statement of faith comes in. Applying the standards of the Announcement of Autonomy accurately has permitted us to make up for ourselves and our set of experiences when we have gotten sidetracked.

There is no American personality without the American statement of faith. Notwithstanding, the patriots are right around a certain something, in recommending that the American personality is something other than about a bunch of thoughts. These thoughts are lived in our way of life — that is valid. It is likewise obvious, as Lincoln said about his well-known "spiritualist harmonies of memory," that our normal experience and our normal history structure an extraordinary story. A story encapsulates the genuine lives and connections of individuals and a common social involvement with a common existence in history that we call the US.

The sharing of involvement with existence — all by itself — isn't normal for what some other country encounters. At the most fundamental level, indeed, I would agree that all countries are in that regard the same. In any case, what made it different for Lincoln was that he accepted and he trusted that the "better holy messengers of our temperament," that was grounded in the American statement of faith, would contact the spiritualist harmonies of memory that make up that story — and that's what it was "contact" that put us aside from different countries.

Allow us to end by making two focuses.

One, how much public traditionalism sounds conceivable lays on a significant verifiable misconception. Proclamations all by themselves that sound valid and, surprisingly, appealing must be suspended in a condition of verifiable amnesia to check out.

At the point when Hazony says, "Public union is the mysterious fixing that permits free establishments to exist," it makes a practically clear commonplace point, at least for the nations that are as of now free. The issue starts when he connects this with the overall practice of the excellencies of patriotism as an idea. Then, at that point, it gets truly chaotic.

Is public attachment the mysterious fixing to free establishments to patriots in Russia? In China? Or on the other hand in Iran? Scarcely. Patriotism in these nations is the unpleasant foe of free establishments. On the off chance that the response is, "All things considered, we don't imply that sort of patriotism," the inquiry gets truly asked: Why offer expansive general expressions about patriotism by any means assuming the special cases loom so enormous? On the off chance that the special cases turn out to be the standard?

Our subsequent point is this. On the off chance that this was only a scholastic discussion over the possibility of patriotism, we guess it truly wouldn't be all that significant. You could allow the intelligent people to divide their hair and antiquarians to come to their meaningful conclusions about the historical backdrop of patriotism, and you could take a brief trip and see whether the idea of patriotism truly helps us strategically — regardless of whether it's valid.

the issue is greater than that for preservationists. The moderate development today faces tremendous dangers to our most fundamental standards. From the left, we face reformists who have consistently said that our statement of faith and our cases to American transcendence was a cheat. They have consistently contended that we were a country like some other. The more revolutionary of them contend that we are more regrettable than different countries unequivocally because our establishing standards were founded on lies.

Presently, we face another test on the sacredness of the American statement of faith from an alternate heading. This time, from the right. It starts things out by obscuring the differentiations between patriotism as really rehearsed and the uniqueness of American transcendence. Then, at that point, it proceeds to raise the apparition of the country state similar to a thought — on the off chance that not the focal thought — to American traditionalism. That is the same as what a mainland European moderate most likely would agree about their practices.

American preservationists, to be perfectly honest, have one or two serious misgivings of the public authority. They have one or two glaring misgivings of the country state. That makes us preservationists. So why raise the idea of the country express that is so unfamiliar to the American moderate practice?

the response might have to do with the more deeply philosophical change that is happening inside a few moderate political circles. It is presently becoming in vogue for certain preservationists to scrutinize private enterprise and the unrestricted economy. Some are in any event, contending that there are currently no restricting standards to what the state and the public authority can or ought to do for the sake of their political plan.

This used to be designated "enormous government" traditionalism. It was considered then to be a liberal recommendation, it is, in my view. It imparts a disturbing guideline to present-day reformism. Where it counts, having the public authority as opposed to individuals settle on significant conclusions about their lives is, on a fundamental level, the same as a gradual contending for the requirement for the government to end destitution and dispense with imbalance.

That's what the thought is, with preservationists responsible for government, this time it will be unique. This time we will ensure that the public authority that we control will drive interests in the correct bearing, and we will settle on the ideal choices on what the compromises are.

Does this sound recognizable? Don't protectors of enormous government generally contend that this time it will be unique?

Set to the side briefly whether we preservationists could at any point control such an administration to adequately do our desired things it to do. Would we like to enable an administration significantly more in modern and different sorts of financial and social strategy that will without a doubt utilize that exceptionally expanded ability to obliterate the things that we cherish and trust about this country?

The most effective way, to safeguard America's significance, its extraordinary cases, and its personality may be, is to have confidence in what made us extraordinary in any case. It wasn't our language. It wasn't our race. It wasn't our nationality. It wasn't our modern arrangement. It wasn't the force of government to choose what the compromises are. It wasn't in an administration that concludes what sort of work is honorable or what sort of work isn't. What's more, it unquestionably wasn't a confidence in the country state or the significance of patriotism.

It was our statement of faith and the conviction framework that was represented and lived in a culture, our establishments of common social orders, and our popularity-based method of government that made America the best country throughout its entire existence, everything being equal. In a word, it was our confidence in ourselves as decent and free individuals. That made America extraordinary. That made us a free country. Furthermore, it keeps on doing so today.

Chapter 3:Understanding Patriotism Through Examples

Numerous instances of patriotism remember circumstances for which a country meets up for a particular reason or in response to a critical occasion. Investigate a few distinct models seen over the entire course of time.

In the Skirmish of New Orleans when the Americans beat the English, Andrew Jackson turned into the "Legend of New Orleans" and supported Americans' feeling of predominance over England.

India's advancement of India as a Hindu country is an illustration of patriotism. It calls for everybody to stick to Hindu standards although there are tremendous religions in the country.

Donald Trump's "America First" crusade was viewed as a type of patriotism since it pushed American standards on others and prohibited explicit societies.

Hitler's solidarity with the Germans through different strategies to accomplish his plan is a verifiable illustration of patriotism.

Patriotism is apparent in European nations' provincial development. The Europeans attempted to push their contemplations and belief systems on different nations, some of the time forcibly.

The solidarity of the Soviets while carrying their country to implode after the Virus War is a presentation of patriotism in ongoing history.

The solidarity of the Serbian minorities in Croatia and Bosnia prompted ethnic purifying.

Scotland chose a patriot party in 2007.

In 2007, Grains effectively chose another patriot party. The motivation behind the party was to advance the Welsh language and customs.

Images, for example, the Association Jack and melodies like Rule, Brittania! are instances of the appearance of patriotism in Britain during the 1700s.

The Greek Conflict of Freedom was started by Greek patriots as a demonstration of joined insubordination.

The unification of the Turkish talking people groups in Focal Asia called Container Turkism was a philosophy of Turkish patriots.

Vladimir Putin's attaching Crimea from Ukraine, and "Russia against the world" manner of speaking is an illustration of patriotism.

Aryanism, a philosophy that expresses that Aryans are the expert race, has been viewed as a type of, or a part of, patriotism.

The Japanese, during WWII, showed patriotism. The Japanese world-class attempted to show their prevalence and attempt to rule others.

Benito Mussolini is an illustration of a nationalistic pioneer.

Keeping Canada's dairy industry neighborhood is an illustration of financial patriotism since it focuses on the monetary interests of Canadian residents.

As these models show, patriotism can be utilized for good purposes or for terrible purposes relying on what the country meets up to achieve.

Chapter 4:Perspectives of Patriotism

There are two points of view about patriotism's beginning: primordial and innovator:

primordialist - This recommends that patriotism is the consequence of people's transformative propensity to accumulate and join in gatherings. Pierre van sanctum Berghe is an essential defender of the primordialist point of view.

innovator - This recommends that patriotism is exceptionally new, and its presence requires contemporary cultural and social development. Henry Maine, Max Weber, and Ferdinand Tonnies are a portion of the unmistakable innovator scholars. The principal utilization of "patriotism" is ascribed to Johann Gottfried Herder in the last part of the 1700s.

Checking Patriotism out

Patriotism can be a strong method for accomplishing objectives as a country. Patriotism can likewise be an instrument of control by the initiative of a gathering or country and can prompt grave viciousness. Now that you know a piece about patriotism, you should investigate extremist legislatures

"Patriotism is war," François Mitterrand proclaimed in 1995, as a determination to a long discourse setting out the targets of the French administration of the European Association. Expressed in a setting of European reconciliation, then, at that point, taken up again by many French legislators, including François Hollande and all the more as of late Emmanuel Macron, in response to the ascent of the super right, this relationship among patriotism and war should be figured out in the West as the immediate result of the two universal conflicts that undeniable the twentieth hundred years. Since it enlivened the tactical systems that we know in Germany, Italy, and Japan, patriotism has from that point forward been disparaged by an entire age, brought into the world during or directly following WWII.

Besides the fact that patriotism no longer appears to address an untouchable for the new ages, however, the ascent in force of outrageous conservative gatherings and libertarian developments throughout the course of recent years likewise appears to highlight a resurgence of this philosophy —all the more egregious as it corresponds with the downfall of the conventional ideological groups in numerous Western nations.

Nonetheless, the patriotism we are seeing today isn't equivalent to that of the 1930s. It takes on various structures, at various territorial and public levels, which it appears to be applicable to attempt to comprehend and characterize, in its different implications, starting with one political and social setting and then onto the next.

Historical framework

Introduced as "one of the most remarkable political powers of the 20th hundred years", patriotism is an international reality that permits us to figure out numerous circumstances and many contentions in this present reality (Radiator and Berridge 2016). Without a doubt, it has prompted numerous reconfigurations of the political space following the two Universal Conflicts and the Virus War (Brubaker 1996-4).

Brought into the world in Europe with the "Individuals' Spring" of 1848, patriotism was created as an outcome of the Congress of Vienna (1814-15), which had decided to disregard the liberal and public yearnings of individuals. In Italy, Belgium, Ireland,

Greece, Hungary, and Poland, the dismissal of the government by unfamiliar administrations created and appeared as a patriot disturbance in pretty much vicious structures. Giuseppe Mazzini, in Italy, was a critical figure in this development, while John Stuart Factory ("Contemplations on Delegate Government", 1861) and Ernest Renan ("What is a Country?", 1882), a couple of years after the fact, endeavored to hypothesize the subject of what comprises a country.

The country states consequently developed countries –groups of individuals sharing a typical attachment– compared to this state from a patriot philosophy pointed toward legitimizing the presence of that equivalent country (Gellner, Hobsbawn, and Thiesse, 1999). They did not just comprise the getting sorted out standards of the world but the premise of global relations also (Rosière 2020, Reece 2016).

Toward the start of the 21st century –the period we propose to zero in on, country states are confronting a progression of social and financial difficulties in a setting of disintegrating personalities and social interconnection made by globalization. They see their sovereign powers disintegrating and are changing, or dread they are changing, into "post-public" states (Habemas 2000) while the political space they administer no longer compares to the financial space that rises above public boundaries.

Euroscepticism, doubt of migration, and, in the US, dismissal of multilateralism and the arrival of protectionism are in this manner leading to a resurgence of patriotism, frequently in a forceful, nativist, and egalitarian structure.

In the meantime, different peculiarities are thusly fuelling territorial patriotism, for which the relationship with the extreme right no longer works since they are politically cross-over in social orders like Catalonia, Scotland, the Basque Nation, Flanders, Quebec... European reconciliation then, at that point, more unexpectedly, Brexit, the Coronavirus pestilence, have all been deciding components in the scrutinizing of country states from stateless countries which, since they have seen the – relative or emotional – the disappointment of pluri-public states, are deciding to battle politically for their autonomy.

We are in this manner seeing patriotism on a few levels: state patriotism –sometimes oblivious, what some call "commonplace", or "regular patriotism", and territorial patriotism, which challenges the boundaries of country states to provide for a few social countries –or stateless nations– their State.

Theoretical considerations

Whether a country is viewed as a separating factor (Bekus, 2010) or as an "envisioned local area" (Anderson, 1993), the bond that joins individuals from a similar country involves banter among researchers. From one perspective, some accentuate ethnocultural understandings, characterizing the premise of the country from genuine attributes like culture, language, history, or belief system (Adams in Bekus 2010).

Then again, others offer pioneer understandings, which consider the country to be a cognizant development, secured in the present and free of the past (Bekus, 2010). Teachers likewise have their methodology with, from one perspective, history specialists, who break down patriotism as political power and, then again, ethnologists, who will generally fabricate it around the thought of nationality (Löfgren in Martigny 2010).

Moreover, patriotism questions borders, which are introduced by Michel Foucher as a focal gadget in the creation of countries (Foucher 2012). Since it should have a topographical premise –a express, a country, and a domain should correspond (Kassem 2012, Foucher 1991)– the country state model arose alongside the idea of boundary. Even better, borders were the regional switches to legitimize country states and were then instrumentalized to build up public opinion. Since the boundary is "the envelope of the country" (Foucher) yet additionally a "marker of personality" (Piermay, 2005), considering this connection between state, country and border are suitable.

Patriotism is likewise a shape-moving peculiarity: whether it is comprehensive or restrictive, ethnic or municipal, supportive of state or hostile to state (Kassem et al 2012), every development, contingent upon its cases, modalities, and establishing standards, fits distinctively into these classifications. Sequentially, there is a distinction between the patriotism that has come about because of the "nationalization of the political space" and the patriotism that delivered it (Bubaker 1996). Eventually, are these thoughts still significant? Or on the other hand, have types of "neo-patriotism" arisen?

Objectives

Since patriotism previously arose in Europe before being "sent out" to the New World through the country state model and in a setting of colonization, the peculiarity will be moved toward relatively.

Europe, most importantly, winds up in the grasp of contradictory powers: the craving to construct a supranational substance that would supersede country states or worldwide states, the development of sovereignism in light of European reconciliation, yet additionally the rise of territorial patriotism that interest to make their state - Catalonia, Scotland, Flanders... Is this an indication of a Europe in an emergency? What significance would it be a good idea for us to provide for these patriot developments?

Additionally, not all European nations have stuck to the country-state model. The Unified Realm, similar to Belgium, are worldwide - or plurinational - a state made out of a few countries, characterized by Stéphane Pierré-Covers as "various networks, each mindful of its particularity and showing the longing to safeguard it" (Pierré-Covers 1995). During the 1980s, Euroscepticism rose and patriotism became more grounded inside nations (for example the Scottish patriots' interest for a country state). On the off chance that a few substances wish to frame a state based on a patriot development, is this not confirmation that the country state has a brilliant future? Could the European Association turn into an association of country states? Isn't the imaginable European salvation that could emerge out of stateless countries in light of a principal contradiction between the two?

The Americas, as far as it matters for them, have taken on the country state model conflicted, in a setting of decolonization, through pretty much vicious cycles relying upon the country. Similarly, they have followed the model of European reconciliation, setting up territorial arrangements like NAFTA, MERCOSUR, or CARICOM. Be that as it may, these endeavors at territorial reconciliation have confronted critical obstructions, including the refusal of states to surrender what they view as hard-won public autonomy.

Subsequently, these arrangements are more economic accords, with no supranational aspirations, that advance more utilitarian than institutional reconciliation (Sohn et al, 2007).

Additionally, patriotism has been connected to native or Indianist developments in exceptionally ongoing times. For instance, Bolivia, which is a plurinational state, has been stood up to with personality and regional cases by "local" people groups, which the public authority has generally considered as populaces possessing a domain.

Latin American patriotism is additionally to be broken down with regards to battles between political specialists and native networks, who were the initial casualties of this provincial patriotism through the spoliation of land and the subsequent deforestation that has been tremendously talked about in Brazil for instance...

At long last, whether it is the state, ideological groups, or common society that ingrains and constructs patriotism by revitalizing around images and standards, patriotism is the product of specific entertainers who produce a specific talk - the public story or political projects - whose point is to prepare people around this "association" that joins the country.

It is these inquiries concerning the various types of patriotism that mark the start of the 21st century that this gathering wishes to investigate by organizing them around the accompanying tomahawks:

The principal pivot will look at the connection between patriotism and populism. The libertarian developments that have duplicated in Europe and the Americas instrumentalize "conventional" or "customary" patriotism through an enemy of migration and support of power talk. Any

proposition on the connection between patriotism and migration or patriotism and power applies to our appearance. How could patriotism be instrumentalized by egalitarian talks advancing withdrawal? What vision of the country is advanced? What is the spot for novices in the public undertaking? Are the talks that are arising in Europe and the Americas comparative?
A subsequent pivot will zero in on the resistance between territorial patriotism and state patriotism.

Moving toward the subject from various angles will be capable:
As a matter of some importance, recommendations investigating the particularity of territorial patriot developments and their cases toward the start of the 21st century will be special. Are these developments the consequence of a political issue between the focal state and a district or is it rather an issue of a social (and "public") union inside the locale? Is the

feeling of territorial having a place - seen as "public", subsequently an issue of definition - viable or not with the public having a place (of the country state)?

Besides, when we realize that Quebec, Basque, Catalan, Corsican or Flemish independentists went to Scotland in 2014 to go to the freedom mandate, we can likewise concentrate on the presence of transnational fortitude connections between specific patriot developments, especially among Europe and the Americas, when the Scottish Public Party has won the decisions (2021) by an embarrassing margin and is fruitlessly requiring another mandate.

At long last, when we know the job that dialects have played in the development of patriotism (Brunet-Jailly 2017), recommendations that will look at how dialects have been placed at the assistance of patriotism in the 21st century will likewise be gladly received. One could imagine the significance given to Gaelic and

Ulster Scot in the discussions preceding the reclamation of a gathering in Northern Ireland in 2020, the endeavors of the Scottish patriot government to have Scots perceived as a public language (not vernacular), but rather models proliferate, for example, the ongoing change of Bill 101 in Quebec managing the French language. The job of Catalan and Basque in comparing patriotism is likewise totally principal as a public definition around the language question.

Then again, in Latin America, aside from Portuguese, every one of the nations share Spanish as an authority language, regardless of whether Guaraní in Paraguay or the pre-Colombian dialects in Bolivia are currently co-official. Does language construct the country? Might a country at any point be multilingual? Could a similar country at any point ride a few states (and in this manner be transborder)?

A third pivot will zero in on patriotism and the redefinition of boundaries in a setting of regionalization and reconciliation, whether in Europe with the European Association or in the Americas with territorial partnerships.

Does the European project stamp the start of the emergency of the country state with the deficiency of specific public images (money, borders)? Is the European Association a space of co-power? What relations does the European Association wish to lay out between the country states and the supranational establishments? Does European development prompt the coming of a European personality and maybe even a European country?

Does European citizenship contend with public citizenship? The EU likewise gives a job and a voice to the districts of the country states, as entertainers in the execution of European strategies. Is the country state (in

Europe in any event) still the best entertainer in a globalized 21st hundred years?

Has the EU looked to debilitate the country states? Has a Europe of districts been genuinely thought to be an option in contrast to a Europe of country states? How might Brexit at some point be a mise en abyme for the Scottish or Catalan independentists (Catalexit)?

These reflections could likewise, according to a relative perspective, make it conceivable to look at the connections that structure the country states and the American territorial groupings: the previous NAFTA, MERCOSUR, the Focal American Reconciliation Framework or CARICOM (the Caribbean People group). Albeit less cultivated than the European Association, do these groupings convey a personality aspect that could provoke - or be contrary to - existing public characters? At long last, what will happen to these territorial groupings when populism is on the ascent? Since patriotism is at the intersection of disciplines, this gathering expects to be both cross-over and transdisciplinary. All approaches are gladly received, whether they connect with human advancement, topography, history, political theory, worldwide relations, social science, etymology, ethnology, brain research... The moderators are additionally urged to embrace multidisciplinary and relative philosophies to think about European and American nations.

Chapter 5: These Are the 3 Types of American Patriotism

Contemplate your relationship to your nation of origin. It's most likely genuinely confounded, isn't that so? Probably, there are a few things you like about it, a few things you think could be better, etc. Some of the time this intricacy gets a piece lowered. In the US, for instance, we're frequently given personifications of thoughtless, banner-waving extremists from one perspective and "hostile to American" nonconformists on the other, however as a general rule nearly everybody is in a tremendous center.

As a general rule, there are shades of patriotism (an expansive term characterized, pretty much, as "enthusiastic sentiments") that are about something other than how enormous a fan you are of your nation of origin...

As Bonikowski and DiMaggio contend in their paper, there's something of a hole in the social science writing concerning American patriotism: The vast majority of the surviving exploration hasn't moved toward the subject according to a reasonable point of view on how people intellectually process a major, chaotic idea like a country in their minds. "There hasn't been a lot of commitment with patriotism as a bunch of overall mental designs, as social organizations of convictions through which individuals figure out the country," Bonikowski tells Study of Us. At the point when we think of the US, it sets off a snare of related ideas — that is, in addition to some point on a "like/disdain" scale.

To attempt to acquire a superior, more nuanced comprehension of Americans' connections to their nation, Bonikowski and DiMaggio took a gander at a few classifications of General Social Overview reactions from 2004: questions having to do with respondents' degree of nationalistic self-distinguishing proof, pride, exorbitant arrogance, and "ethnocultural and municipal standards for public participation" (that is, inquiries concerning who considers a "genuine" American).

By utilizing a measurable procedure called dormant class examination, they had the option to lump the respondents into bunches that were genuinely comparative — that is, bunches that would in general respond to such inquiries in some ways. Four such classifications jumped out, three of them patriot and the other less so (they're summed up in this realistic, which is too enormous to even think about implanting yet which pleasantly makes sense of how every classification was comprised):

-**Enthusiastic patriots** are, it might be said, your exemplary banner falters. Comprising 24% of the example in

Bonikowski and DiMaggio's review, they were more probable than any of different gatherings to "feel exceptionally near America," to "report being 'extremely glad for every one of the 10 possible wellsprings of pride,'" and to "unequivocally concur with each of the five proportions of public arrogance." In light of their reactions to the inquiries concerning being a genuine American, "a greater part saw Jews, Muslims, freethinkers, and naturalized residents as something not exactly 'real American.'"

-**The separated** were the littlest gathering in the example, containing only 17% of the example. The specialists gave the gathering this name because its individuals "kept the most grounded underwriting of even the most generally held patriot convictions and opinions, since they proclaimed especially low degrees of pride in state establishments, and because they seemed to cease from discount commitment with a public personality." Just 21% of them, for instance, "detailed feeling exceptionally near the country, contrasted with 56% until the end of the example." These people simply aren't all that nationalistic, in the ordinary feeling of the word.

-**Prohibitive patriots** "communicated just moderate degrees of public pride however characterized being 'genuinely American' in especially exclusionary ways." This was the biggest gathering in the example, at 38%, and its individuals were just moderate in their degrees of public distinguishing proof, pride, and over-the-top arrogance, while nearly as prohibitive as the Ardents when it came to who does and doesn't consider a "genuine" American. This is a fascinating blend we'll get back to.

-**Creedal patriots** complied with a "type of public self-understanding related with a bunch of liberal standards — universalism, a vote-based system, and law and order —

some of the time alluded to as the American statement of faith." They made up 22% of the example, communicated high levels of pride in the U.S., and were receptive about what it intended to be an American.

Donald Trump appears to be a great deal like a Prohibitive. He has, generally, shunned standard official discussion about how extraordinary America is.
Rather, Trump has zeroed in on what he sees as the nation's long, steep descending slide. In the Trumpian view, the US has been overwhelmed by unlawful foreigners and lawbreakers and is truly self-destructing.

The country needs a resilient man (or a strongman) to assemble it back once more, and some portion of that strength comes from perceiving that main certain individuals can be genuine Americans. "It shows up there is a few comparabilities between the profile of this gathering as far as the perspectives toward the country and what we see among Trump allies: ethno-social prohibition, alongside a low degree of pride in the state," says Bonikowski, however, he was mindful to add that it was impossible to demonstrate, in light of this information, that Trump draws excessively from Restrictives

Perhaps There are Some except Political Reality taking a look at All things considered Why It Took Sociology Years to Address a Straightforward Mistake About 'Psychoticism'

There's a fascinating catch, however — while white Restrictives might well comprise a portion of Trump's critical coalition of help, there are likewise a lot of dark and Latino Restrictives who, while underwriting a similar general classification of patriotism, arrived for altogether different reasons and who are probably not going to be Trump allies. African-Americans were "unequivocally overrepresented" in this gathering, the specialists composed — 68% of the African-American respondents in the example fell into this gathering, for instance, and they were for the most part leftists. Their general absence of pride in and distinguishing proof with America most likely comes from a different spot: Much of the time, it could originate from despondency about how the U.S. has treated racial minorities, said Bonikowski. In this way, zoomed out, these dark and Latino Restrictives appear to be like their white partners, in that they answer specific inquiries in comparative ways, however, their governmental issues are presumably altogether different.

Bonikowski and DiMaggio additionally took a gander at information from a similar overview in 1996 and 2012, and they saw something fascinating when it came to how those years contrasted from 2004:

Notwithstanding the significance of patriotism for governmental issues and intergroup relations, sociologists stand out enough to be noticed the peculiarity in the US, and history specialists and political clinicians who in all actuality do concentrate on the US have restricted their concentration to explicit types of patriot opinion: ethnocultural or community patriotism, positive energy, or public pride. This article enhances, first, by looking at a surprisingly expansive arrangement of measures (from the 2004 GSS) tapping public distinguishing proof, ethnocultural and municipal standards for public participation, space explicit public pride, and harmful correlations with different countries, subsequently giving a more full portrayal of Americans' public self-understanding.

Second, we utilize inactive class investigation to investigate heterogeneity, apportioning the example into classes portrayed by unmistakable examples of perspectives.

Traditional differentiation between ethnocultural and community patriotism portrays pretty much 50% of the U.S. populace and doesn't represent the out-of-the-blue low degrees of public pride found among respondents who hold prohibitive meanings of American nationhood.

A subset of fundamentally more youthful and knowledgeable Americans misses the mark on serious areas of strength for one of enthusiastic opinion; a bigger class, essentially more established and less knowledgeable, embraces each type of patriot feeling. Controlling for sociodemographic attributes and hardliner distinguishing proof, these classes fluctuate fundamentally in perspectives toward ethnic minorities, migration, and public power. At long last, utilizing practically identical information from 1996 and 2012, we find underlying progression and distributional change in public feelings over a period set apart by psychological oppressor assaults, war, financial emergency, and political conflict.

American patriotism — the complex of thoughts, feelings, and portrayals by which Americans figure out the US and their relationship to it — has to a great extent been the territory of U.S. history specialists and political psychologists.

The previous have fundamentally centered around minutes when American statehood was dangerous: the principal long stretches of the Republic and the period after the Nationwide conflict (Kohn 1957; Waldstreicher 1997). In a couple of special cases (e.g., Citrin et al. 1994), the last option has inspected pieces of the peculiarity — positive energy, public personality, closed-mindedness — disregarding their relationship. Although sociologists have made focal commitments to academic writing on patriotism (Brubaker 1996; Calhoun 1997; Gellner 1983; Tilly 1994), they have frequently stayed away from the U.S. case.

However, by practically any definition, the US is no more interested in patriotism. Researchers have perceived the effect of patriot thought in both governmental issues and regular day-to-day existence (Billig 1995; Calhoun 1997; Lieven 2004; Smith 1997), and history specialists have chronicled its moving characteristics after some time (Waldstreicher 1997; Zelinsky 1988).

Political patriotism energized military development during the period of Inevitable success, and a surprisingly impressive feeling of public power has driven U.S. political pioneers to dismiss worldwide administration structures, from the Class of

Countries to the Kyoto Accord. At the degree of regular day-to-day existence, Americans treasure public images — most outstandingly the banner — to a degree surprising in cutting-edge majority rule governments (Collins 2004). What's more, in ongoing U.S. political missions, clashes over the country's significance, from its treatment of foreigners and strict minorities to its legitimate job on the world stage, have activated enormous fragments of the electorate.

What makes sense of this insightful disregard? Much exploration on patriotism centers around subnational nonconformist developments, which have been to a great extent missing from U.S. governmental issues since the finish of the Nationwide conflict. Research likewise will in general focus on unequivocally ethnocultural patriotism, though community patriotism — a patriotism of shared esteems as opposed to shared nationality — has overwhelmed

U.S. public talk (however see Smith 1997). Patriotism is much of the time a weapon of the distressed — bunches that have lost regional control of their countries or countries crushed in war. History's victors have less justification behind harshness and more ability to approach discusses. As Billig (1995:55) puts it, "'Our' patriotism isn't introduced as patriotism, which is hazardously unreasonable, excess, and outsider. Another personality, an alternate mark, is found for it. 'Our' patriotism shows up as 'positive energy' — a valuable, fundamental, and, frequently, American power."

We accept that the disregard of American patriotism is lamentable for three reasons. In the first place, the U.S. case is critical according to a relative point of view, because of the US's unmistakable situation as "the principal new country" (Lipset 1963), its endurance as a multiethnic and multiracial commonwealth of more than a few centuries, its status as a worldwide hegemon, and the noticeable quality of municipal patriotism in the American "common religion" (Bellah 1967). Contrasted with most European countries, public ethnocultural claims have been moderately muffled in standard post-Bellum talk (with outstanding special cases, similar to the official missions of George Wallace, Patrick Buchanan, and Donald Trump), yet Canadian-style multiculturalism gets little help.

Second, understanding how Americans envision, feel about, and converse with each other about their country is a fundamental yet conventionally overlooked essential to getting a handle on political conflict in the late-20th and mid-twenty-first hundreds of years, about which sociologists and political researchers have composed so a lot (Baldassarri and Gelman 2008; DiMaggio, Evans, and Bryson 1996; Fiorina, Abrams, and Pope 2005). As Tracker (1991) contends, members in social conflict frequently base their contentions on convictions about the suitable extent of the state's relationship to the individual; the limits (or deficiency in that department) among government and other social establishments; and standards for authentic participation in the public commonwealth.

Third, understanding American patriotism for its possibly game-changing impact on the U.S is basic. governmental issues and international strategy and, through those impacts, on the job the US plays on the planet (Lieven 2004). Understanding how Americans think about their country might give hints with regards as far as possible political pioneers face when they arraign unfamiliar conflicts or look for worldwide collaboration, as well as proposition knowledge into public reactions to psychological oppressor assaults and into social inspirations that impact citizens' political decisions.

Our motivation is to look at American patriotism as it is communicated in light of overview things on perspectives connected with the country and public personality. In light of past work, we accept that more than one adaptation of patriot thought coordinates Americans' relationship with their country.

We utilize dormant class examination (LCA) to distinguish four subsets of respondents overviewed by the Overall Social Review (GSS) in 2004 who fluctuate methodically in their reactions. We attract on a hypothesis to choose disposition things to remember for our investigation, however, our methodology likewise has a critical inductive part: as opposed to expecting that respondents stick to intelligible philosophies that can be distinguished and deduced, we use LCA to recognize unmistakable sorts of patriotism without assuming their intelligent consistency (Bonikowski 2016a).

In the wake of describing the attitudinal organization of the dormant classes and breaking down the corresponding class task, we investigate whether class participation is related autonomously to perspectives toward minorities, migration, public limits, and international strategy, net of the effect of sociodemographic measures and hardliner distinguishing proof.

At long last, we affirm that the construction of the classes yielded by the 2004 investigations additionally fits information from 1996 and 2012, and we then, at that point, think about the dissemination of the classes over the three waves to evaluate the transient dependability of American perspectives toward the country state.

This book makes a few unmistakable strategic commitments, which thusly yield a few novel considerable discoveries. Though most overview put together investigations of patriotism center concerning a restricted scope of convictions, we investigate perspectives on four components of patriotism at the same time: public distinguishing proof (sensations of closeness to the country); standards of public participation (what makes somebody "genuinely American"); pride in the country's legacy and unambiguous establishments; and public arrogance (convictions involving frequently harmful examination between the US and different nations).

We prohibit perspectives toward strategy issues like migration and financial protectionism that, albeit conceivably connected with perspectives on nationhood, are not constitutive of those perspectives.

Our own is the principal investigation of American perspectives connected with patriotism to utilize inactive class examination to distinguish gatherings of respondents with unmistakable examples of overview reactions. LCA is intended for cases in which the noticed appropriation of some arrangement of factors mirrors the blending of at least two heterogeneous gatherings. Not at all like component investigation, which bunches factors that are related to each other across a whole example and doles out consistent variable scores to individual perceptions, LCA tracks down discrete arrangements of respondents with unmistakable blends of perspectives (McCutcheon 1987). Since past work on U.S. patriotism declares there are unmistakable methods of public self-understanding (Schildkraut 2011; Smith 1997), LCA is particularly appropriate to this examination issue.

Our understanding is driven by a hypothetical structure that sees disposition reactions as reflecting fundamental schemata — connected portrayals comprising a mental system through which data is handled — putting together the space of ethnicity (Brubaker, Loveman, and Stamatov 2004; DiMaggio 1997). We guess that individuals fluctuate not just in the specific perspectives they hold, but in their understandings of the relationship among these mentalities, in the full of feeling loadings of the portrayals, these perspectives bring out, and in associations between the country construction and other schemata, including that of oneself.

This view drives us to involve LCA to approximate the distinguishing proof of mental subcultures (Zerubavel 1997; cf. Baldassarri and Goldberg 2014); and, having distinguished them, to look at how each example of perspectives toward the country is related with sees on migration and other arrangement issues.

At long last, we exploit the planning of the 2004 GSS, which was handled soon after the US's intrusion and resulting control of Iraq and under three years after the assault on the World Exchange Community, and of the way that similar things were remembered for public overviews in 1996 and 2012. This makes it conceivable to investigate change after some time in both the construction of patriot perspectives and their dissemination during periods in which patriot opinions were pretty much liable to be persistently actuated.

These developments yield considerable discoveries that extend how we might interpret Americans' connections to their country. In the first place, consolidating LCA with an extraordinarily expansive scope of pointers uncovers that respondents in 2004 partitioned into four classes: two outrageous classes, described, separately, by exceptionally high and moderately low degrees of the underwriting of a wide range of patriot cases; and two fewer limits, however unmistakable, middle of the road classes. Individuals from the principal bunch have exceptionally prohibitive perspectives on the stuff to qualify as "genuinely American" but relatively unobtrusive degrees of public pride. Individuals from the subsequent gathering show elevated degrees of public pride, however a moderately comprehensive meaning of American personality, underwriting not many limitations to genuine participation.

Second, our investigations uncover that conflict about the significance of Christianity as a standard of public participation is a focal pivot of division among our respondents. To be sure, religion, alongside race and schooling, is an exceptionally critical indicator of a class task in our models.

Third, we exhibit that inactive class participation predicts perspectives toward migration and other social issues, even in the wake of controlling for an extensive variety of sociodemographic factors and ideological group distinguishing proof. At the end of the day, understandings of public participation are connected with a sectarian association, however, they likewise display free relationships with a scope of political perspectives.

At long last, our examinations show that the construction of patriot opinions as uncovered by LCA remained moderately stable somewhere in the range of 1996 and 2012, even as the overall size of the classes changed, especially in 2004. In synopsis, underneath an overall agreement on the excellencies of the US, Americans contrast extraordinarily in the degree of their nationalistic sentiments and the personality of their public self-understandings, in manners that are significant and powerful to political change.

Paradoxically, Brubaker (2004:10) characterizes "patriotism" not as a first-class philosophy or a particular arrangement of standardizing convictions, yet as a space: "a heterogeneous arrangement of 'country'-situated figures of speech, practices, and conceivable outcomes that are persistently accessible or 'endemic' in present-day social and political life." We take on this more extensive definition since we wish to comprehend how a large number of perspectives that comprise respondents' country schemata — from affection for nation and contentiousness toward untouchables to basic commitment to the country — are disseminated, how they answer outside occasions, and how they connect to different mentalities and strategy inclinations.

We utilize more unambiguous terms (distinguishing proof, participation standards, pride, and over-the-top arrogance) to allude to the substance of these perspectives.

Chapter 6: Patriotism in the United States

Researchers have come to acknowledge the view that at least two understandings of country and citizenship coincide and contend inside U.S. political culture, however, neither students of history nor overview investigators settle on the number and nature of these perspectives.

Smith (1997) contends that U.S. political culture has been molded by three practices: a liberal custom that underscores all-inclusive privileges and independence; a municipal conservative practice that spotlights local area self-administration and aggregate freedoms and commitments; and an ethnocultural custom that mirrors the white populace's craving for proceeded with a predominance (with the meaning of "white" developing with progressive influxes of migration) (cf. Walzer 1990). Different creators have recognized two fundamental flows: a public story that verbalizes municipal upsides of universalism, the obligation to the country, levelheadedness, resistance, correspondence of chance, and law and order; and a xenophobic counter-account, frequently connected with moderate Protestantism and the practice of Jacksonian patriotism (Lieven [2004] expresses this position particularly successfully; see likewise Blum 2005; Kaufmann 2000; Spencer 1994). Citrin and partners (1994) add to the creedal and nativist points of view a third, multicultural, meaning of American nationhood.

Observational investigations of American patriotism (and firmly related subjects like positive energy) frequently use factor examination to distinguish clashing subjects in Americans' public self-understanding. In light of an overview of understudies, Schatz and partners (1999:153) recognize "blind nationalism" ("an unbending and unyielding connection to country, portrayed by unquestioning positive assessment, steadfast faithfulness, and narrow-mindedness of analysis") from "productive enthusiasm" (described by "addressing and analysis of current gathering rehearses that are driven by a longing for positive change") (see likewise Parker 2007). Consolidating center gathering records and overview information, Schildkraut (2002, 2011) certifies the presence of Smith's (1997) three types of public belief system, adding a fourth, "incorporationism," that portrays the US as a foreigner country persistently reinforced by the implantation and digestion of progressive influxes of transients.

We add to this examination custom by coordinating investigations of dissimilar signs of patriotism and utilizing a scientific methodology that finds philosophical examples in gatherings of respondents, as opposed to in bunches of factors. In particular, we use information from the

2004 General Social Overview (enhanced in one segment by practically identical information from the 1996 GSS and a 2012 GfK Custom Exploration review) to resolve a few inquiries that stream from this writing. How do the classifications of American patriotism that arise when reactions to an expansive scope of overview things are exposed to inactive class investigation contrast with the kinds of patriotism placed by past examinations?

What sociodemographic, political, and philosophical attributes anticipate the task to each class? How much do respondents relegated to various classes fluctuate in their social perspectives and public-arrangement inclinations past what one could expect in light of their sociodemographic attributes and sectarian responsibilities? Lastly, how powerful are these attitudinal designs over the long run?

Data

Information for the fundamental investigations comes from the 2004 Public Personality Supplement to the GSS, which was controlled mutually with the Worldwide Social Overview Program. The GSS is a full-likelihood, individual meeting overview intended to screen changes in friendly qualities and perspectives. It has been directed every year, and later bi-every year, by the Public Assessment Exploration Center beginning around 1972. During the 1980s, the GSS started including effective modules researching explicit regions in more noteworthy profundity than the continuous center overview licenses (Davis and Smith 1992).

In the wake of checking on 31 freely accessible datasets containing things connected with the estimation of patriot perspectives and opinions (Bonikowski 2008), we picked the GSS information since they are the most over the top total in the number of components of patriotism canvassed and in the reach and nature of covariates, and because the GSS is the most broadly approved and powerful public attitudinal review in the US. Additionally, because similar inquiries were posed in 1996 also as 2004, we can think about the construction and content of patriot opinions when the September 11 assaults.

Our investigation centers around four parts of American patriotism: public distinguishing proof, standards of public participation, public pride, and public arrogance.
We talk about every individual arrangement of measures.

National identification
Public distinguishing proof — the significance of public character comparative with different parts of individual personality — is a focal piece of numerous originations of patriotism. Verifiable records of

American patriotism (Kohn 1957) have underscored the basic significance of the shift from the transcendence of state distinguishing pieces of proof to ID with the public government in the beginning of the Republic; and the country battled a Nationwide conflict to choose the supremacy of public versus territorial ID (Faust 1988). As indicated by Citrin and partners (1994:2), "patriotism is effective when it overshadows accessible elective foci of connection like family relationship, religion, financial premium, race or language." GSS respondents were inquired, "How close do you feel to your [town or city; state; America; North America]." Respondents were about two times as reasonable (51%) to report feeling "exceptionally close" to "America" than to some other district or political unit.

Criteria of legitimate membership

Most records of American patriotism respect replies to the subject of "Who is an American?" (or in the phrasing of the GSS, who is "genuinely American") as denoting the distinction between the creedal (or community) and ethnocultural customs (Lieven 2004; Smith 1997; Walzer 1990). The previous hugs the liberal statement of faith of resistance and universalism, though the last option draws solid limits in light of attributes like origination, language, religion, and race. By and large, the US has wavered between the receptiveness to newbies recorded on the Sculpture of Freedom, from one perspective, and intermittent episodes of nativist prohibition on the other (Higham [1955] 1983).

Zeroing in on "qualities that emotionally characterize participation in a specific political local area," Citrin, Reingold, and Green (1990:1128) track serious areas of strength for down among an example of Californians for creedal progressivism, yet significant help, too, for the striking nature of etymological and strict standards.

An expansive agreement arose among 2004 GSS respondents around the significance to being "genuinely American" of American citizenship, capacity to communicate in English, feeling American, and "regarding America's political establishments and regulations," with dominant parts calling these "vital" and with north of 90% accepting these were "genuinely significant" or "vital." Less respondents respected being "brought into the world in America" or having "lived in America for the vast majority of one's life" as vital, however these standards got significant help in any case, with more than three of four respondents choosing "reasonably" or "exceptionally" significant.

Respondents were more partitioned in their perspectives on the centrality of Christianity to public participation: a majority (48 percent) picked "vital," however the following most well known reaction, from 18% of respondents, was "not vital." Generally speaking, 65% revealed that Christianity was a reasonably or vital standard, though 35% chose "not vital" or "not significant by any stretch of the imagination."

National pride

Citrin, Wong, and Duff (2001) characterize public pride as fundamental to positive energy (which they view as firmly connected to patriotism). Pride is unique concerning however connected with distinguishing proof, in that close-to-home satisfaction from the accomplishments of a substance increment with the emotional vicinity of that element to oneself. As Smith and Kim (2006:127) put it, "Public personality is the durable power that the two holds country states together and shapes their associations with different states. Public pride is the good influence that the public feels towards their nation, coming about because of their public personality."

GSS respondents were most glad for the US's military, history, and logical and mechanical accomplishments: over around 50% of the example portrayed themselves as "exceptionally pleased" of each, with more than 90% "very" or "to some degree" pleased. Different wellsprings of pride were accomplishments in sports and accomplishments in craftsmanship and writing (more than 90% to some degree or exceptionally pleased), how a majority rules government works (89%), the country's financial accomplishments (87%), and its international impact (78%).

Respondents appraised two things lower: fair and equivalent treatment of all gatherings (75%) and the government-managed retirement framework (only 56%).

National hubris

Word references characterize "closed-mindedness" as a type of positive energy that is outrageous in degree and involves pride in one's gathering as well as declarations of predominance over others.

We keep away from the term as a result of serious areas of strength for its implications, rather utilizing "over the top arrogance" to portray a bunch of things that reflect public pride in the US overall and that certifies an inclination for the US contrasted with different countries (or, in one case, an unrestricted perspective on residents' commitments on the off chance that the US conflicts with different nations).

We utilize the vast majority of the actions that Smith and Kim (2006) allude to as "general" pride (rather than "space explicit"). This development is additionally predictable with Citrin and associates'

(2001:74-75) differentiation between "positive energy" ("sensations of closeness to and pride in one's nation and its images") and "closed-mindedness" ("a limit and limited unwaveringness, the confidence in one's nation's predominance, whether it's set in stone").

Various creators venture to such an extreme as to compare these actions with patriotism in general. Williams ([1951] 1970:490), in an exemplary text on U.S. society, characterized patriotism as "the conviction that U.S. values and establishments are the absolute best on the planet" (see additionally De Figueiredo and Elkins 2003).

Five GSS concur/differ things tap this component of patriot conviction and opinion. Two proclamations reflect decisions that, while harmful, are not expressive of moral predominance: "America, by and large, is a preferable country over most different nations," and "I would prefer to be a resident of America than of some other country on the planet." The first could be valid if "better" alludes to specific standards on which the US is moderately exceptionally positioned (e.g., law and order or common freedoms). The second could be propelled by unadulterated personal responsibility as opposed to moral assessment. These perspectives got broad help, with 90% of respondents underwriting the last option and 80 percent concurring with the previous.

Things in the subsequent pair are all the more straightforwardly characteristic of sensations of public predominance: "The world would be a superior spot on the off chance that individuals from different nations were more similar to Americans," and "Individuals ought to help their nation regardless of whether their nation is off base." as opposed to the principal pair, concurrence with these two assertions was undeniably more estimated. Only 42% revealed wishing that individuals from different nations were more similar to Americans, with a majority setting themselves at the midpoint of the five-point scale. Just 37% supported the perspective on "my nation right or wrong," with 41% protesting this position.

At long last, a fifth thing estimates how much "there are things about America that cause me to feel embarrassed." Albeit the inquiry doesn't unequivocally evoke an examination between the US and different nations, sensations of disgrace in the nation suggest some outside reference point from which the respondent delivers that judgment. Among the GSS respondents, 26% didn't feel embarrassed about the US, and 56 percent felt embarrassed (the leftover 18% picked the middle-of-the-road reaction classification, neither concurring nor contradicting the inquiry brief).

Implementation of Latent Class Analysis

We start by utilizing inactive class investigation (LCA) to distinguish classes (subsets of respondents) with unmistakable reaction designs across all the overview things estimating patriot perspectives. LCA, which we carried out utilizing the Inactive Gold 5.0 programming bundle (Vermunt and Magidson 2005), is an information decrease technique that gauges an unnoticed ostensible gathering variable (where each worth compares to a discrete "dormant class") that records for the covariance between the noticed pointers.

Utilizing most extreme probability and the Newton-Raphson technique, the model at the same time appraises different boundaries under the presumption that the pointers are autonomous of each other and restrictive on the inactive class variable. An LCA model that predicts the noticed reaction design y utilizing an inactive class

111

variable X with T values has the accompanying likelihood structure (Bakk, Tekle, and Vermunt 2013:276):

$$P(Y=y)=\sum t P(X=t)P(Y=y|X=t)$$

Given the neighborhood freedom presumption, which places that the K pointers are autonomous inside each inactive class t — that is, the joint likelihood of a given reaction design is a result of individual thing reaction probabilities — the last option term of the situation can be reworked as follows (Bakk et al. 2013:276):

$$P(Y=y)=\sum t P(X=t)\prod k P(Yk=yk||||X=t)$$

The boundaries to be assessed by the LCA model incorporate the overall class extents, $P(X=t)$, and the reaction profiles for each class, $P(Yk=yk|X=t)$.

We exploit three augmentations of the fundamental inactive class model. In the first place, notwithstanding the center patriotism pointers, our model incorporates sociodemographic covariates, which produce a more precise task of perceptions of dormant classes (Clogg 1981; Hagenaars 1993).

This methodology, otherwise called "multinomial logit inactive class relapse," at the same time models two sorts of restrictive probabilities: the dissemination of patriotism pointers contingent on dormant class participation, and the reliance of inert class enrollment on sociodemographic covariates (Yamaguchi 2000).

Second, because practically speaking most LCA models don't impeccably fulfill the neighborhood autonomy presumption, it is feasible to work on model fit by considering nearby conditions between a portion of the pointer factors, as well as between certain markers and covariates (Vermunt 1997). (In LCA speech, "pointers" allude to the constitutive factors that are utilized to characterize the classes, and "covariates" are auxiliary factors that assist with further developing class tasks.) The conditions that most seriously influence the model can be effortlessly distinguished by looking at the bivariate residuals once the model has been assessed. The sets of factors with the biggest residuals can then be determined as together ward in a resulting model.

Third, we utilize a recently evolved technique for the examination of distal results (i.e., subordinate factors) in the LCA demonstrating structure.

Previously, if specialists had any desire to anticipate different factors utilizing respondents' dormant class participation, they would initially gauge the idle class model, then, at that point, produce back probabilities of class enrollment for every respondent and, at long last, in a different third step, relapse the results of interest on those back probabilities — a training scrutinized for creating seriously descending one-sided gauges and erroneous standard blunders (Bolck, Murmur, and Hagenaars 2004).

Ongoing strategic developments, be that as it may, have made it conceivable to address characterization mistakes (by which a few respondents are defectively doled out to the classes) in the three-step cycle to produce unprejudiced evaluations (Bakk et al. 2013). We utilize this procedure while looking at the connection between patriotism and strategy inclinations.

The fundamental LCA models incorporate the pointers portrayed as well as a bunch of sociodemographic covariates that incorporate age, schooling, pay, orientation, race, district, strict division, legalism, birth in the US, and party distinguishing proof. We regarded the attitudinal pointers as ordinal with the end goal of the investigation. After the cancellation of perceptions with missing information on sociodemographic covariates, the example size was 1,077. We picked a four-bunch arrangement in light of decency of-fit measurements and interpretability. For additional subtleties on question phrasing, unmistakable measurements, model determination, and the treatment of missing information

Varieties of American Popular Patriotism

We describe the substance of each class concerning class-explicit probabilities of reactions to the 23 patriotism pointers. Of the four classes, two were outrageous — outstanding for high and low qualities on the vast majority of the patriot things. Two others were less effortlessly put on a continuum of pretty much nationalistic: one characterized "genuine American" in an exceptionally prohibitive way but communicated moderately low degrees of pride in American establishments and achievements; the other communicated elevated degrees of pride and characterized participation in a substantially more comprehensive manner.

Ardent Patriots

Individuals from the bigger of the outrageous classes (24% of all respondents), whom we call the enthusiastic patriots, were more probable than individuals from some other class to feel exceptionally near America; bound to say it was "vital" for a genuine American to have every one of the seven qualities about which respondents were asked; probably going to report being "extremely pleased" of each of the 10 possible wellsprings of pride, and more probable than some other to concur or unequivocally concur with every one of the five proportions of public hubris.

Even though the enthusiastic patriots scored most elevated on each component of patriotism — distinguishing proof, participation standards, pride, and over-the-top arrogance — they were not unpredictable in their reactions. Vast dominant parts saw every standard of being "genuinely American" as "vital," practically completely supported citizenship, capacity to communicate in English, feeling American, having lived in America a large portion of one's life, and regarding establishments and regulations, however, less accepted a genuine American needed to be brought into the world in America (86%) or be a Christian (75 percent). In any case, a greater part saw Jews, Muslims, rationalists, and naturalized residents as something not exactly "genuinely American."

Essentially every one of the enthusiastic patriots announced being "exceptionally pleased" with America's military, history, and accomplishments in science and innovation.

Significantly less communicated extraordinary pride in the nation's fair and equivalent treatment of all gatherings (51%), its political impact on the planet (48%), or its government-managed retirement framework (28 percent). Other pride things in the middle between. Each individual from this class communicated an inclination toward being a resident of the US and everything except six concurred that

America is a "superior country" to most others. Almost 66% (64%) felt the world would be a superior spot on the off chance that individuals in different nations were more similar to Americans, and only 50%, even of this most nationalistic gathering, accepted individuals ought to help their nation on the off chance that it is in the wrong. More enthusiastic patriots than individuals from some other class (43%) were unashamed of any parts of America.

the run of the mill individual from this class was a white male perceptive Outreaching or Mainline Protestant with moderately minimal conventional schooling, living in the South. The enthusiastic patriots were eight years more established than the rest of the example, with a mean age of 51. They had respectably low livelihoods and were almost certain that others had suspended their tutoring after secondary school. Strategically, the enthusiastic patriots were probably going to self-distinguish serious areas of strength for as and were among the to the least extent liable to self-recognize as liberals.

The minority who self-distinguished as liberals were more established and had even lower salaries than their conservative partners; they were additionally less inclined to recognize as white or as Protestant, to live in the South, or to report having no religion. They were, be that as it may, practically the same as far as orientation and probability of having been brought into the world in the US.

There is proof that in any event, some enthusiastic patriotism is related to military assistance. Even though information on veteran status was not accessible, 18% of men in the enthusiastic patriot class (contrasted with somewhere in the range of 5 and 8 percent in different gatherings) announced that they had a place with veterans' associations.

The disengaged

The other outrageous class was the littlest, making up 17% of the example. It comprises of what we call the "separated" — separated from the country since they kept the most grounded underwriting of even the most generally held patriot convictions and feelings, since they maintained especially low degrees of pride in state establishments, and in light of the fact that they seemed to forgo discount commitment with a public personality. The most grounded proof for the last derivation comes from reactions to the public ID thing: just 21% of respondents in this gathering announced feeling exceptionally near the country, contrasted with 56% until the end of the example. They were additionally to the least extent liable to underwrite any trademark as "vital" for being "genuinely American," frequently by significant spaces. For example, simply half appraised as vital the capacity to communicate in English, which 89% of different respondents saw as constitutive of being genuinely American. Indeed, even citizenship was named "vital" by only 47%. Different standards, for example, being Christian, being brought into the world in the US, or having lived in the US for the vast majority of one's life, were supported as vital by less than one of every six.

Withdrawn respondents were additionally more outlandish than individuals from different classes to communicate elevated degrees of public pride. A portion of these outcomes recommend a pessimistic assessment of the US's presentation on components of the public statement of faith: only 10% detailed being "exceptionally pleased" of how American majority rules government functions; 7% communicated extraordinary pride in equivalent treatment of all gatherings; 20% communicated pride in American history; and just two individuals communicated solid pride in the country's political impact. Be that as it may, they additionally communicated lower levels of pride in fields like science and innovation (42%) and expressions and writing (31%), where American accomplishments ostensibly have been certifiably critical.

Such examples recommend these respondents were not just reproachful of the US on certain aspects, however they additionally distinguished less unequivocally with the country as a general rule, investing wholeheartedly in American accomplishments in light of the fact that their ethnicity was connected less near their healthy identity. Of course, the separated were additionally to the least extent liable to underwrite any of the over the top arrogance things.

Who were these most un-nationalistic Americans? With a mean age of 38 years, they were the most youthful of any class. African Americans and respondents in the "other" race classification were overrepresented in their positions, as were respondents brought into the world external the Unified States.

Exceptionally taught and less strict respondents were especially liable to have a place with this gathering, and practically undeniably were leftists (with just seven detailing a conservative sectarian connection). This class was tracked down in large numbers in the Upper east and the Pacific West; scarcely any lived in the South or the Mountain West.

As far as religion, Outreaching Protestants and Catholics were underrepresented in this class; Jews and respondents who picked "no religion" and "other" religion were overrepresented. Albeit the livelihoods of the separated were the most minimal of the four classes, this is a component of their young age; among respondents who were 25 or more established, the mean pay of the withdrew surpassed that of prohibitive and enthusiastic patriots (however not creedal patriots).

Just shy of 10% of respondents relegated to this class didn't hold U.S. citizenship, and another 6% were unfamiliar conceived citizens.17 (Almost 50% of non-residents in the example were delegated separated, contrasted with pretty much 14% of the unfamiliar conceived residents.) It isn't is actually to be expected that non-residents would fall into this class.

The unfamiliar conceived are status-conflicting — the individuals who were delegated withdrawn were exceptionally instructed and moderately generously compensated, yet additionally 62% non-white, overwhelmingly non-Christian, and, obviously, rookies to the US. Five percent of the separated were second-age Americans, however multiple quarters were neither foreigners nor offspring of outsiders. The local conceived individuals from this class were knowledgeable, youthful, moderately almost certain than respondents allocated to different classes to be non-white, and probably going to portray their strict confidence as "none" (36%) and their political connection as liberal (80%). At the end of the day, the separated class blends a moderately little arrangement of prosperous foreigners whose perspectives might mirror an absence of distinguishing proof with the US with a lot bigger arrangement of generally youthful and knowledgeable local conceived respondents who favor leftists and are frequently (however not solely) individuals from ethnoracial or strict minorities.

Restrictive nationalists
Not at all like the enthusiastic patriots and the separated, the two leftover classes didn't fall into a monotonic continuum from more to less nationalistic.

They were, be that as it may, moderate in altogether different ways. One class, which we call the prohibitive patriots, comprised of respondents who communicated just moderate degrees of public pride, however, characterized as being "genuinely American" in especially exclusionary ways. The other class, which we call creedal patriots because their profile of perspectives recommends constancy to the American statement of faith of liberal universalism, comprised of respondents who communicated elevated degrees of public pride close by a hesitance to qualify "genuinely American" with numerous solid circumstances.

We start with the previous: the prohibitive patriots, who were the biggest gathering, comprising 38% of the example. Individuals from this gathering were moderate in their public distinguishing proof and embraced unobtrusive degrees of public arrogance (not exactly either the enthusiastic or creedal patriots): 94% liked to be U.S. residents, 79% concurred that there could be no greater country than the US, 43% concurred that individuals in different nations ought to be more similar to Americans, and 38 percent embraced the view that one ought to help one's nation in any event, when it is off-base. Just 18% announced never encountering disgrace in the US.

Prohibitive patriots were likewise like, albeit less limited than, the enthusiastic patriots in putting conditions on who ought to be considered to be a "genuine American." Well over half unequivocally supported the view that no one but Christians can be "really American"; almost three of every four accepted it is "vital" that a "genuine American" be brought into the world in the US or have lived in the US for the vast majority of one's life, and 69 percent saw regard for American political establishments and regulations as vital for being genuinely American.

Given their elevated degree of help for prohibitive standards of public participation, shockingly couple of individuals from this class announced being "exceptionally pleased" with American accomplishments.

Without a doubt, their reactions to the pride questions were nearer — generally speaking, a lot nearer — to those of the separated than to those of the enthusiastic patriots or creedal patriots. Dominant parts communicated extraordinary pride just in America's military and its set of experiences. On the other hand, only 13% announced being exceptionally pleased with the American majority rules government, and only 9% communicated extraordinary pride in America's worldwide political impact.

Who were these respondents who characterized genuine Americans so prohibitively yet manifested such low degrees of public pride? Unpleasant speculation would portray them as Americans who are distraught concerning a blend of race, orientation, or social class. Ladies were overrepresented among the prohibitive patriots; normal livelihoods were the second most reduced of the multitude of classes, and a moderately little level of these respondents proceeded with their schooling past secondary school. African Americans were unequivocally overrepresented in this class (68% were doled out to this gathering), as were Hispanics.

Dark Protestants were additionally addressed on a huge scale (significantly more so than in some other classes), as were Fervent Protestants. As anyone might expect given their standards for "genuine American" status, moderately few were brought into the world external the US. Strategically, Freethinkers were unequivocally overrepresented (close to a portion of the Freethinkers in the example were in this class), recommending an inclination toward the confined class by the politically estranged. Albeit moderate liberal and conservative identifiers were almost similarly liable to be relegated to this class, unequivocally hardliner conservatives were underrepresented (the vast majority of them were found among the enthusiastic and, less significantly, creedal classes), and serious areas of strength for though were overrepresented, mirroring the different financial positions and racial organizations of these two gatherings.

By far most of the African Americans in this class were leftists, although 14 of the 18 African American respondents who pronounced themselves conservatives were allocated to this classification. Conversely, Hispanic respondents who related to the Progressive alliance were underrepresented and the people who related to the Conservative Association were overrepresented in this class. Generally speaking, it appears to be reasonable that this type of patriotism reflects resentment more than philosophy.

Given the surprising unmistakable quality of African Americans among prohibitive patriots, we verified whether these outcomes were curios of the more unfortunate task of non-whites to inactive classes because of a blend of more modest numbers with conceivable model heterogeneity.

We in this manner thought about mean individual-level class task probabilities for blacks and whites in every one of the four classes. The outcomes show that the distinctions in the accuracy of characterization by race across the four classes are minor. On account of the prohibitive class, the mean characterization probabilities for dark respondents are higher than those for white respondents.

Creedal Patriotism

Creedal patriotism alludes to the type of public self-understanding related to a bunch of liberal standards — universalism, a vote-based system, and law and order — some of the time alluded to as the American statement of faith (Hartz 1964; Lieven 2004; Lipset 1963).

The class of respondents we call creedal patriots, which represents 22% of the example, fits this profile more appropriately than some others. Their type of patriotism was high on public pride however put not many limitations on who can profess to be "genuinely American." Creedal patriots displayed elevated degrees of public distinguishing proof, with 65% detailing that they felt "exceptionally close" to America, a rate practically identical to that of the enthusiastic patriots. They were more outlandish than the enthusiastic patriots to report being "exceptionally pleased" with

American accomplishments, however, bound to do as such than either prohibitive patriots or the separated. 57% communicated extraordinary pride in the "manner in which a majority rules government works," contrasted with only 13% of the prohibitive patriots, and 67 percent communicated pride in America's financial accomplishments. They matched the enthusiastic patriots in pride in science and innovation, with 82% announcing significant levels. Like everything except the separated, they unequivocally supported the thoughts that America is a preferable country over most and that being a resident of the US is better.

Even though they didn't score as high on the over-the-top pride factors as did the enthusiastic patriots, a majority concurred that the world would be better on the off chance that others were more similar to Americans and that one ought to help one's nation regardless of whether it is off-base.

Like the enthusiastic patriots, they were additionally significantly less reasonable than prohibitive patriots or the separated to feel embarrassed about America.

The distinctions between creedal and prohibitive patriots are particularly apparent in their reactions to the inquiries concerning the characteristics that are vital in making somebody "genuinely American."

They were almost certain than the prohibitive patriots (85 versus 69 percent) to say that regard for American establishments and regulations was vital. Conversely, scarcely any respected being a Christian (21 percent), having been brought into the world in the US (16%), or having lived here the vast majority of one's life (20%) as vital standards. At the end of the day, albeit the creedal patriots separated between levels of Americanness, not at all like the prohibitive patriots they didn't do as such based on credited qualities.

Who were these a little more than one of every five Americans whose sees most firmly approximated what is purportedly the American statement of faith? Generally, they were people upon whom destiny had grinned.

They were in all probability of any gathering to hold postgraduate educations and to have graduated school; their mean pay of $78,582 was right around 40% higher than that of the following most affluent gathering (the enthusiastic patriots). Predictable with their financial prosperity, they were excessively conservative, nearly so much so as the enthusiastic patriots (even though with less solid hardliners).

They were almost certain that some other gathering to have been brought into the world external the US (23%), and the vast majority of the unfamiliar brought into the world in this gathering had U.S. citizenship.

Not very many were African American or distinguished as Dark Protestants.

This class likewise incorporated the biggest portion of respondents who characterized themselves as racially other and as Jewish, with Catholics very much addressed (comprising 28% a strict majority) however Protestants, particularly Evangelicals, were less inclined to be doled out to this gathering. Territorially, creedal patriots were overrepresented in the Pacific and Mountain states and underrepresented in the Upper east and South. At the end of the day, creedal patriotism is, somewhat, the philosophy of people for whom the Pursuit of happiness has worked.

Generally speaking, be that as it may, their foreigner starting points, strict confidence, racial personalities, or territorial areas place them on the outskirts of what is much of the time addressed as the American standard. We suspect this blend of financial accomplishment with true-to-life insignificance delivers a proclivity for a comprehensively comprehensive comprehension of the country.

It is outstanding how little cross-over we see between patriotism and hardliner situation among the two mediocre gatherings. (The predominance of conservatives among the enthusiastic patriots and of liberals among the separated better matches got intelligence.) To guarantee that the overrepresentation of conservatives among creedal patriots was not a relic of the model, we separated the individual-level class task probabilities by party distinguishing proof for every one of the four classes. These outcomes, show no measurably tremendous contrasts like characterization by a party in any of the classes, filling in as additional consolation that the LCA model is accurately determined and the party results precisely mirror the data.

We additionally inspected the foundation attributes of the conservative creedal patriots (see the internet-based supplement, Contrasted with their Popularity based partners, they varied outstandingly in their strict foundations (almost 50% of the leftists were Catholic and 16 percent were Jewish, contrasted with 22% and 6 percent, separately, of conservatives, though 36% of conservatives and only 13% of liberals doled out to this class were Protestant), foreigner status (with 50% of leftists however just 17% of conservatives brought into the world external the US), racial distinguishing proof (87% of the conservatives were white, contrasted with 69% of the liberals), and orientation (with 45% of the conservatives and 58 percent of the liberals being female). In different regards the two gatherings were comparative.

Contrasted with different conservatives, those relegated to the creedal patriot class were less inclined to live in the South;

significantly more reasonable than conservative restrictives or ardents to report their confidence as "other" or Jewish (26% contrasted with 9 and 10 percent, separately); and impressively bound to have been brought into the world external the US (17% contrasted with 3% for restrictives and 7 percent for ardents).

At the end of the day, the creedal conservatives, albeit more like conservatives than creedal liberals, were more similar to leftists than different conservatives — more assorted, less Southern, and less traditionally religious.

Chapter 7: Summary

The inactive class investigations yielded four classes of the respondent. Two of these were outrageous, one portrayed by elevated degrees of public distinguishing proof, prohibitive perspectives toward public participation, elevated degrees of public pride, and elevated degrees of over-the-top arrogance; and one described by something contrary to these.

Individuals from the previous were excessively more established, less taught, white Outreaching conservatives residing in the South, though the last option consolidated exceptionally instructed, generously compensated foreigners and youthful, profoundly instructed, mainstream leftists from the coasts. Between the two limits, two classes showed up more firmly lined up with the differentiation between ethnocultural and creedal patriotism (see, e.g., Lieven 2004;

Smith 1997) (even though it is essential to take note that our actions stretch out past standards of public participation). Prohibitive patriots were excessively female, African American or Hispanic, Outreaching or Dark Protestant, low in schooling and pay, and brought into the world in the US. Creedal patriots were exceptionally instructed and major league salary, probably going to dwell outside the South, and included moderately a couple of Protestants and the biggest extent of foreigners.

Notwithstanding a few distinctions, there were striking similitudes in segment profiles between the prohibitive and enthusiastic patriots and between the separated and creedal patriots. One could conjecture — we can do no more — than restrictives were potential ardents for whom the Pursuit of happiness didn't emerge. One could likewise conjecture that the creedal patriots, and less significantly the separated, were respondents for whom the Pursuit of happiness emerged, and for whom negligibility from ethnocultural meanings of American personality (by race, confidence, or home) prompted reception of patriotism that embraces people such as themselves or, on account of the withdrew, to a dismissal of patriotism altogether.

The presence of the outrageous classes is an original tracking down not expected by past examination, similar to the low degree of public pride among a subset of Americans who hold ethnocultural originations of the country. These highlights of American patriotism became noticeable here because of the expansive scope of pointers remembered for this examination and the limit of LCA to disconnect subsets of respondents with unmistakable reaction patterns. 41% of Americans in 2004 had public self-understandings that reflected wide nostalgic directions to the country as opposed to fine-grained philosophical segregations, to such an extent that they either embraced or dismissed (separately) pretty much every component of a prohibitively enthusiastic patriotism.

On the other hand, the greater part of respondents fell into bunches predictable with — yet additionally more mind-boggling than — recently noticed types of American patriotism. Undoubtedly, a few examples were normal to all classes — a general need put on citizenship and communicating in English contrasted with different warrants of "being genuinely American;" more noteworthy pride in America's accomplishments in science and innovation than in its government-managed retirement framework; and more eagerness to underwrite the recommendation that American citizenship is ideal over all others than to support the guideline of "my nation right or wrong." However, the distinctions are striking.

Is Patriotism connected to Social Perspectives and Strategy Inclinations?

Put another way, does patriotism matter? Is it related to Americans' perspectives on significant social issues or with their strategy inclinations, so that knowing Americans' mentalities and opinions toward the country empowers us to foresee these different perspectives more successfully than we could dependent just upon data about their age, orientation, instructive fulfillment, race, a nation of birth, strict confidence, legalism, district of home, pay, or ideological group identification?

This test represents a high obstacle. On the off chance that various sorts of patriots fluctuate fundamentally after we control for this large number of different variables, we might construe, first, that our LCA examination distinguished components of conviction that are related with an expansive range of conviction and assessment; and second, that notwithstanding the consistent ideas, the gatherings are definitively different in their perspectives.

the net relationship of patriot class task with 17 perspectives: sees on arrangements connected with racial and ethnic minorities; mentalities toward migration; perspectives toward the remainder of the world and to multiculturalism; and international strategy sees addressing U.S. sovereignty. Higher qualities on the reliant factors compare to more moderate (i.e., hostile to redistributive, against foreigner, protectionist, and noninterventionist) perspectives.

The controls referenced before are remembered for all models however are not shown for clearness. Creedal patriotism is the overlooked class to which different classes are thought about, however, in examining our outcomes, we every so often draw on different correlations also. Every one of the models utilizes a three-step ordinal-logit LCA model for distal results with rectification for misclassification (Bakk et al. 2013).

Impact of Class Membership on Social and Policy Attitudes with Controls

Past exploration gives us much motivation to guess that how individuals might interpret the country would be related to perspectives connected with in-bunch/out-collective vibes (Tajfel 1982) and worries about friendly limits and custom entrance (Douglas 1966), like perspectives on race, migration, exchange, worldwide relations, and public power (Citrin et al. 2001; Kunovich 2009).

A few researchers have found proof of a relationship between perspectives connected with patriotism and perspectives on intergroup relations. Citrin, Reingold, and Green (1990) track down that what they call "Nationalism" predicts perspectives toward foreigners and migration more successfully than do segment measures or even openness to apparent danger. Simultaneously, various types of patriot conviction and opinion might have contrasting ramifications for perspectives toward out-gatherings.

Parker (2007), in an examination of California's Field Survey, reports that "visually impaired positive energy" ("America right or wrong") was connected with negative perspectives on racial and strict minorities, though what he calls "representative nationalism" (connection to enthusiastic images and center American qualities) was related with open and embracing reactions. Li and Brewer (2004) report that exploratory subjects prepared with requests to bunch fortitude, aggregate interest, and great citizenship communicated elevated degrees of resilience; though subjects prepared with messages that underscore intergroup contrasts supported moderately more dictator and antagonistic positions. It might follow from this view that over-the-top arrogance and a prohibitive perspective on participation in the public local area would impact mentalities uniquely, in contrast, to do public distinguishing proof and pride in America's accomplishments (see likewise De Figueiredo and Elkins 2003).

Policies related to ethnic and racial minorities

Like the investigations looked into above, we track down critical net relationships of specific types of patriotism with a scope of perspectives. Indeed, even with broad controls, the separated were more steady in multiculturalism and related positions than were individuals from different classes. Predictable with their help for municipal meanings of a "genuine American" and their low qualities on over the top pride, the separated were substantially more reasonable than others to underwrite the view that the public authority ought to "regard and safeguard the privileges of minorities" and that it is better if minorities "keep up with their unmistakable traditions and customs." Despite their comprehensive perspectives on the standards for public participation, creedal patriots didn't contrast fundamentally from enthusiastic patriots in their reactions to either thing tapping mentalities toward multiculturalism.

Furthermore, even though they were bound to say that administration ought to help minority privileges than were prohibitive patriots, they were less so than the separated. Strangely — and to some degree shockingly — enthusiastic patriots were almost certain than creedal patriots to help the government help for safeguarding minority societies.

Attitudes toward immigrants

We would anticipate patriot feelings — particularly opinions about the country's limits — to be related to perspectives on foreigners (Bail 2008), and they were.

Prohibitive patriots were fundamentally almost certain than creedal patriots and the separated to accept that foreigners increment crime percentages and remove occupations from Americans, and they were essentially more probable than creedal patriots, the withdrew, and enthusiastic patriots to differ that migration is useful to the economy and that outsiders further develop society by acquiring groundbreaking thoughts and societies, as well as to concur that there is an excessive amount of government spending on movement.

Enthusiastic patriots were additionally fundamentally almost certain than creedal patriots (and generally speaking, the separated) to concur that foreigners cause wrongdoing and remove American positions, that outsiders shouldn't hold similar privileges as residents, and that all the more should be finished to forestall unlawful migration.

However a prohibitive perspective on public participation was not essential to basic perspectives on migration: creedal patriots were likewise fundamentally more probable than the separated to concur that movement removes Americans' positions, increments crime percentages, and consumes an excess of government spending, as well as to differ that foreigners further develop society by getting groundbreaking thoughts and societies. They were likewise almost certain that separated respondents to incline toward extra measures against unlawful migration.

Attitudes concerning America's boundaries

Perspectives toward foreigners are an extraordinary instance of reactions to the infiltration of public limits by individuals, societies, and cash from abroad.

Results here were comparative, with the separated communicating the least understanding, and prohibitive patriots and enthusiastic patriots communicating the most arrangement, with protectionist and noninterventionist sees: the two gatherings were fundamentally almost certain than creedal patriots or the separated to underwrite the perspectives that U.S. TV programming ought to incline toward American substance, that outsiders ought not to be allowed to possess the land in the US, and that the US ought to scale back imports. Enthusiastic patriots showed up significantly more worried than prohibitive patriots with social interruptions from abroad, as confirmed by their more grounded help for the displaying of American substance on U.S. TV.

Foreign policy

Three things center around issues connected with the strength of American sway: an overall assertion declaring that the US ought to seek after its public interest in any event when that prompts worldwide struggle; a thing about the North American International Alliance (NAFTA); and a speculative inquiry concerning whether the US ought to concede global bodies the ability to implement ecological arrangements. Yet again predictable with their high scores on over-the-top arrogance and their impressive pride in state establishments, the enthusiastic patriots were fundamentally almost certain than either the separated or the prohibitive patriots to underwrite the place that the US ought to follow its advantages no matter what, (the separated were essentially less inclined to concur with this view than were the creedal patriots).

The outcomes additionally recommend that creedal patriots were fundamentally more gone against than the remainder of the example to giving worldwide bodies implementation abilities. At long last, the separated were the exceptions on the NAFTA question, showing fundamentally more prominent understanding than others with the explanation that the US doesn't profit from the economic alliance.

A few ends rise out of these investigations. In the first place, even with various controls, the separated and the enthusiastic patriots contrasted fundamentally from creedal patriots on numerous perspectives connected with minorities, migration, and America's connection to the world. Without a doubt, creedal patriots contrasted fundamentally from the separation on 14 of the 17 things that we researched, and from enthusiastic patriots on 10 of 17.

Second, the example of distinction recommends that the prohibitive patriots' distraction with limits, joined with their moderately powerless pride in the country's achievements, sums up negative perspectives on minorities and of foreigners, as well as the dread of numerous sorts of the entrance of the country's limits.

Conversely, the separated respondents' and the creedal patriots' universalistic guidelines for consideration in the American commonwealth, and creedal patriots' solid pride in American accomplishments, militate toward a receptiveness to homegrown distinction and worldwide contact. Given these outcomes, as well as the way that the distinctions we portray are seen in the wake of controlling for hardliner distinguishing proof, it would be a misstep to conflate famous patriotism with political philosophy.

Third, pride in the country's achievements and public distinguishing proof might vaccinate Americans somewhat against the most outrageous types of racial or ethnic prohibition and xenophobia. We see this in the way that enthusiastic patriots were less outrageous on certain factors estimating these aspects than were the prohibitive patriots.

At long last, the outside legitimacy of the classes distinguished by the LCA investigations is upheld by the way that respondents' class tasks were fundamentally connected with an extensive variety of social and strategy positions. These tremendous impacts are seen in the wake of controlling for various sociodemographic factors, ideological group distinguishing proof, and strict confidence.

Was 2004 a run-of-the-mill year for American Patriotism?

In portraying our outcomes, we purposefully utilized past tense to flag that the construction and appropriation of patriot perspectives in our information might be well defined for 2004, the year in which the second Public Personality Supplement to the GSS was controlled. In this segment, we inquire as to whether this was the situation, exploiting the way that the GSS highlighted indistinguishable patriotism inquiries in 1996 and that we had the option to regulate those questions again in 2012 to a broadly delegated test of respondents surveyed by GfK Custom Research.

By contrasting the general thing values in the four classes in 1996, 2004, and 2012, we can evaluate the underlying dependability of Americans' patriot perspectives; by contrasting the level of people relegated with every, we can look at steadiness in the pervasiveness of each kind over the long run.

Past exploration of the effect of significant public occasions on open perspectives gives us the motivation to expect in any event some adjustment of how Americans envision their country in the period covered by our information.

All through U.S. history, nativism and xenophobia have expanded in times of political danger and, less significantly, financial privation (Higham [1955] 1983). Rahn, Kroeger, and Kite (1996) recommend that such emergencies and their portrayal in the media influence the public state of mind (with individual variety accordingly relying upon the degree to which public character is fundamental to individual personality), prompting expansions in the volume of patriot talk and, possibly, to political preparation Predictable with this contention, Perrin (2005) tracked down an expansion in both dictator and hostile to tyrant talk in letters to the proofreader of a North Carolina paper after the September eleventh assaults.

Collins (2012) battles that emergencies like 9/11 have a direct — albeit short-lived — influence on patriot perspectives by strengthening the public connection and expanding unrestricted help for state establishments, delivering "time-air pockets of patriotism."

Considering that our 2004 information was gathered three years after the September 11 assaults and around one year after the U.S. attack on Iraq, we expected to notice expansions in sorts of patriotism that put stricter cutoff points on authentic standards of the public having a place (following research on xenophobia amid emergency) and involve more noteworthy pride in and support for both the country and the express (the "unite behind the banner" impact

[Perrin and Smolek 2009; Willer 2004]). We in this manner expect expansions in prohibitive patriotism and enthusiastic patriotism and subsequent decreases in the level of respondents appointed to either of the different classes.

The post-9/11 changes in patriot convictions are probably going to be impermanent, as recommended by past examination on aggregate distinguishing proof in the repercussions of significant public emergencies (Collins 2012).

We in this manner expect the appropriation of the four classes in 2012 to look like that seen in 1996. It is possible, notwithstanding, that this pattern might be counterbalanced by the effect of the Incomparable Downturn, which started in 2008.
We are to some degree incredulous about these opportunities for two reasons. In the first place, by 2012, the economy was amidst a languid however consistent recuperation

(the NBER dates the finish of the downturn to the second quarter of 2009 [Cynamon, Fazzari, and Setterfield 2013:21]), which probably hosed any past changes in popular assessment.

Second, proof from overview research recommends that financial slumps seldom produce significant changes in everyday political perspectives. In a review in light of GSS information from 1972 to 2010, Kenworthy and Owens (2011) contend that regardless of Americans' intense consciousness of macroeconomic circumstances, the beyond six downturns didn't influence well-known trust in nonfinancial establishments, perspectives toward government, civil rights convictions, or inclinations for redistributive strategies. Considering these discoveries, it appears to be far-fetched that the Incomparable Downturn would have fundamentally reshaped well-known understandings of the country.

To look at the dissemination of classes over the long haul, we ran a to some degree homogeneous LCA model that empowers us to look at all the while variety by year in the substance of classes (i.e., the circulation of pointers inside each class) and the pervasiveness of each class inside the example. The fundamental outcome is that the construction of patriot opinions was powerful over this 17-year time frame, though the pervasiveness of the classes fluctuated outstandingly.

Chapter 8: Conclusions

Significant Discoveries

As far as anyone is concerned, this article embraces the most exhaustive investigation of the most ridiculously complete information containing perspectives on public self-understanding and feeling from a public example of Americans. It is likewise among the first to utilize inactive class investigation, a technique that empowered us to distinguish how blends of perspectives are held by sets of substantial people. Our outcomes certify and broaden a few consequences of past examination, while likewise making disclosures unexpected by a significant part of the current writing.

In supporting the place that there are numerous types of public self-understanding, and that patriot perspectives and feelings have various sources and suggestions for seeing in different spaces, this study combines with and broadens past work.

Our discoveries are generally unequivocally predictable with past exploration in exhibiting that a readiness to put ethnocultural limitations on participation in the public local area and what we call over-the-top pride are related to negative perspectives on foreigners and migration and noninterventionist and protectionist directions toward the remainder of the world.

We expand on this work by exhibiting the net relationship (after broad controls for sociodemographic attributes, strict confidence, and hardliner distinguishing proof) of adherence to unmistakable perspectives on the country with mentalities toward such matters as unilateralism in international strategy, social and financial protectionism, and multiculturalism.

Our discoveries additionally separate from the consequences of past exploration in a few regards. Numerous eyewitnesses of patriotism have noticed the general trustworthiness of such intelligent practices and propensities as ethnoculturalism, liberal patriotism, municipal republicanism, etc — and have additionally seen that factual proportions of individuals' adherence to such perspectives are related (as we most definitely have announced) with mentalities toward minorities, migration, and other social issues.

In this manner, they some of the time expect that such reasonable belief systems map conveniently onto the perspectives of regular people, so one could figure out the well-known governmental issues of patriotism as a challenge, for instance, between individuals who place their confidence in the American statement of faith and the individuals who view America as a white, Protestant republic.

Notwithstanding analysis of this view (see Brubaker 2004), many examinations on friendly perspectives keep on reflecting it.

In this regard, this review advances in utilizing dormant class examination to distinguish inductively examples of perspectives that describe the conviction frameworks of substantial people without serious areas of strength for making about philosophical rationality.

Without a doubt, such examples are much of the time chaotic, contrasted with the philosophical aspects that check out to subject matter experts and eyewitnesses. Our investigation certifies Brubaker's (2004) incredulity about the down-to-earth comprehensiveness and clearness of the differentiation between ethnocultural and community patriotism and gives unequivocal assessments of the restrictions of this view.

We track down that simply over a portion of American grown-ups (the 60% whom we portray as prohibitive or creedal patriots) stand firm on footholds that can be perceived according to this point of view. Almost around 50% of (the 40% whom we portray as enthusiastic patriots and the separated) either indiscriminately underwrite focal fundamentals of both municipal and ethnocultural patriotism (the impassioned patriots) or are simply tepidly dedicated to any type of patriot feeling (the withdrew).

Albeit apparently illustrative of about around 50% of the U.S. populace, the ethnocultural versus creedal differentiation neglects to catch their perspectives dependably. A significant greater part of the creedal patriots underwrites the view that somebody who doesn't communicate in English isn't "genuinely American." And, similar to those in the enthusiastic class, the prohibitive patriots embrace every one of the limitations on the meaning of the "real American" that the overview offers, and not just a spot of the birth, religion, and language (cf. Kunovich 2009). (Obviously, standards of public participation are just a single characteristic that recognizes the four classes: variety in public pride and over-the-top arrogance which isolates prohibitive from enthusiastic patriots and the separated from creedal patriots.)

Our investigation additionally reveals new insight into the segment, political, and strict variables that anticipate the types of patriotism to which Americans stick. Since we center around anticipating tasks to classes as opposed to situating on unmistakable attitudinal aspects, we are, in actuality, attempting to make sense of how viewpoints consolidate and plan onto sets of people who share comparative perspectives. The main discoveries are both positive and negative.

Emphatically, our outcomes highlight solid connections among strict and public personalities in the US. With regards to standards of public participation, the conviction that being Christian is vital to being genuinely American is the disposition that most unequivocally recognizes creedal patriots and the separated (not many of whom hold this conviction) from prohibitive and enthusiastic patriots (the vast majority of whom do).

What's more, strict confidence — particularly, the inclination of Outreaching Protestants to incline toward enthusiastic patriotism — is a significant indicator of a class task. Albeit American students of history have long valued the profound association between confidence in God and confidence in the country (Higham [1955] 1983; Kruse 2015), our examination investigates this association with extraordinary observational particularity.

At long last, we show that patriotism isn't fixed after some time, however, rather its different assortments shift in pervasiveness, apparently in light of broadly significant occasions, like occurrences of homegrown psychological oppression and unfamiliar conflicts.

Notwithstanding these transient moves, the examples of reactions describing the four sorts of patriotism remained moderately predictable across the three overview waves. At the end of the day, Americans' convictions about their country's state connect into unmistakable understandings with what gives off an impression of being a powerful fundamental construction.

The heartiness of the four sorts of American patriotism and their association with strategy inclinations recommend that these attitudinal profiles comprise significant cleavages in U.S. political culture that part of the way cut across sectarian personality.

Our discoveries may in this manner assist with making sense of the accomplishments of political preparation in light of the egalitarian way of talking (Bonikowski and Gidron 2016) combined with nativist and bigoted cases, most as of late exemplified by the official application of Donald Trump. Trump's mission has utilized a specific vision of the country that underscores the predominance of the American public, the ethical defilement of elites, and desperate dangers presented by foreigners and ethnic, racial, and strict minorities, all while drawing a sharp differentiation between the early stage country and its political establishments.

His requires a re-visitation of America's supposed magnificence days reverberated profoundly with a sizeable fragment of citizens in the 2016 conservative official essential, especially individuals who were white, male, less taught, and dwelled outside beachfront metropolitan communities (a

gathering that included conservatives, yet additionally moderate leftists who were qualified to cast a ballot in open primaries) (Tasteless 2016; Cohn 2015).
The philosophical substance of the Trump lobby's talk and the sociodemographic organization of its help base intently look like the qualities of prohibitive patriots and, less significantly, enthusiastic patriots. Straightforwardly interesting to these's comprehension gatherings might interpret America might have been a significant driver of Trump's prevalence, empowering him to assemble based on patriot feelings conservatives for whom his issue positions could have shown up inadequately conservative.

We can likewise guess — however, do no more, given the absence of direct observational proof — about the connection between our discoveries and backing for the Casual get-together development, which rose to unmistakable quality in 2009. As opposed to center Trump allies in the essential, Tea Carousers were ordinarily steadfastly moderate and conservative; they additionally would, in general, be more established, exceptionally strict, for the most part, Outreaching yet additionally Mainline Protestant, unequivocally working class, school taught, and living in networks isolated by race and training (McVeigh et al. 2014; Skocpol and Williamson 2012).

These sociodemographic characteristics look similar to those of the enthusiastic patriots. Besides, the philosophical bases of Casual get-together help reverberate a portion of the convictions we saw among the enthusiastic class: the Tea Carousers' political activism was set off by the Incomparable Downturn (regardless of whether they bear its brunt) and profound contempt of Barack Obama's administration, however, their perspectives were unequivocally formed by a more broad animosity toward minorities and foreigners, suspicion of scholarly elites, a simpleton comprehension of the Constitution (they were solid nationalists, by their definition), and profound feeling of dread toward progressing social changes in the US (Skocpol and Williamson 2012; Willer, Feinberg, and Wetts 2016). Put another way, albeit the Casual get-together started as development in light of financial complaints, its enlistment of allies fitting the shape of enthusiastic (and maybe prohibitive) patriots might make sense of the development's utilization of a patriot vernacular and energetic images to seek after its cases.

These speculations are fascinating, however, a note of watchfulness is expected: our inductive typology is explicitly worried about assortments of patriotism, and not all governmental issues (revolutionary, etc.) are outlined in unequivocally patriot terms. To the degree that political entertainers honor explicit arrangement suggestions or underscore financial uncertainties, their political cases might be symmetrical to patriot convictions in the populace. In this manner, to assess the connection between well-known patriotism and the new ascent of revolutionary governmental issues, one requires further information as well as an exact hypothetical model that associates patriotism with a political way of behaving. Our article lays the preparation for such future examination endeavors.

At long last, we zeroed in solely on the US, however, the ramifications of our scientific methodology might be significant for different nations also. Specifically, the ascent of revolutionary rights gatherings in Europe since the last part of the 1990s has been worked with by dependence on exclusionary types of patriotism joined with the denunciation of political elites (Berezin 2009; Bonikowski and Gidron 2014; Mudde 2007), which has spoken to the populaces most adversely impacted by European supranationalism and neoliberal changes (i.e., local conceived, low-pay, low-schooling, common citizens) (Ivarsflaten 2005; Stylish and Betz 2003).

These political developments might have benefited from patriot cleavages like those we saw in the US. To investigate this chance, the scientific structure created here could be stretched out to relative exploration of inside country variety in patriot convictions . Such exploration can make significant commitments to the insightful comprehension of the ascent of patriot governmental issues across Western majority rules systems.

Limitations

A few contemplations qualify our trust in these discoveries. Albeit the GSS information is the most ridiculously complete we found in a broad survey, they are as yet blemished. We see three fundamental issues.

In the first place, the proportion of public distinguishing proof scarcely gets at what, according to a mental point of view, is the focal issue — the closeness and level of connectedness of the country construction and the self-composition. Fundamental to the thought of patriotism is that obligation to the country takes "priority over accessible elective foci of connection like a family relationship, religion, financial interest, race or language . . . patriotism suggests that participation in the country is the most disparaging of all loyalties" (Citrin et al. 1994:2).

In this manner, the ideal arrangement of things would evaluate not just the level of distinguishing proof with the country, yet additionally the general significance of public and contending types of ID.

Second, the GSS things utilize the expression "America" all through, as opposed to the country's genuine name, the

"US of America" (ordinarily shortened to "US").

The term America is related to enthusiastic melodies ("God Favor America" and "America the Delightful") and images (the American banner), however, it has additionally been an object of analysis locally (both white radicals and African patriots have utilized the adulterated structures, Amerika, Amerikkka, and Amerikkka as terms of harshness) and hemispherically (by individuals who despise the apportionment of the name of two landmasses for U.S. nationals, against the cases of Canadians, Mexicans, and other Latin Americans).
On the other hand, the "US" shows up in government archives and correspondence and is all the more ordinarily utilized in ordinary administrative settings. That's what we suspect "America" is an emotionally charged term that conjures the consecrated site of nationhood, though "US"

is a more unremarkable term that summons the country's disrespectful components. On the off chance that this doubt is right, utilizing "America" as opposed to "the US" in overview things will probably expand levels of patriot excitement for most respondents, and maybe compound negative effects and estrangement for some others.

Third, the GSS "genuine American" series contains more things that tap ethnocultural types of patriotism than municipal patriotism. Liberal patriotism can incorporate obligation to political and racial resilience, as well as regard for establishments and regulations (Citrin, Wong, and Duff 1990). Additionally, the conservative practice (Schildkraut 2002; Smith 1997; Theiss-Morse 1993) recommends that cooperation in the political cycle is a commitment to participation in the public local area. An ideal dataset would incorporate proportions of the significance of political resistance, support for an opportunity of articulation, and political cooperation to capability as a "genuine American."

Beyond Attitudes

Popular assessment overviews give a significant method for understanding the expansive shapes of public self-understanding in a way that can be summed up across an enormous populace. In that capacity, they are irreplaceable in capturing the idea of American patriotism.

Simultaneously, a far-reaching research program on well-known patriotism requires a reconciliation of three spaces wherein patriotism becomes manifest: (1) individual reactions to social overviews; (2) patriot talk and the organization of patriot images in friendly communication; and (3) the pervasiveness of patriot images and prompts (e.g., banner lapels) in the more extensive social climate. To comprehend the interpretation of patriot thoughts into political activity, one should comprehend how occasions trigger variety in patriot talk and the representative climate, and how to change in examples of collaboration and the climate specifically stimulate or deactivate contending originations of country and citizenship.

Until this point in time, social researchers who concentrate on U.S. patriotism have zeroed in more on overview information than on one or the other communication or the representative climate. One restriction of overview-based disposition research, notwithstanding, is that (except for concentrates on utilizing review tests) it conventionally expects those specific understandings are persistently actuated specifically by respondents, so study reactions are in all actuality stable at the singular level.

However the vast majority get it and approach the most comprehensively accessible social understandings of country and citizenship, and in certain individuals, in any event, actuation of elective accounts might remain in relative equilibrium.

So one should request what sorts of occasions and collaborations are probably going to prime and inspire specific adaptations of patriotism. An exploratory examination is valuable in such a manner. Li and Brewer (2004) had the option to evoke critical varieties in political resistance and over-the-top arrogance by outlining inquiries as far as communitarian versus essentialist thoughts of cultural participation. An exploratory examination is additionally valuable in uncovering parts of schematic association that work during programmed comprehension, however, which might be superseded by the consideration that the overview circumstance evokes. Devotionals and

Banaji (2005), for instance, exhibited that U.S. understudies of all races apparent whites (counting white Europeans) as "more American" than African Americans or Asian Americans, in any event, when they knew nothing about this predisposition.

Direct perception of the social climate is a significant wellspring of understanding also. Billig (1995:6) points out the significance of "commonplace patriotism," the "philosophical propensities which empower laid out countries of the West to be duplicated" through indexical articulations that comprise the state as a reified substance. Eliasoph (1998) and Eliasoph and Lichterman (2003) enlighten how social settings inspire and build up contrasting portrayals of public citizenship. As well as showing the way that patriotism can be as much a component of conditions as of people, such exploration likewise features the interpenetration of community and ethnocultural patriotism (and the trouble, on occasion, of recognizing them) in concrete political talk and activity.

At the end of the day, patriotism is a component of setting as well as individual perspectives. Full comprehension of American patriotism will expect thoughtfulness regarding the convictions and feelings that Americans uncover to overview specialists and the social components that enact specific convictions and opinions specifically settings and incite their transformation into political activity.

Notes

1."Patriotism," a challenged term in the writing, can allude to a large number of ways of behaving, images, and perspectives related to the unavoidable systematization of the country state as a political and social establishment in the cutting-edge world. Numerous political clinicians save the term for prideful or defensive inclinations toward the state, however, we favor a more comprehensive definition that considers the full scope of variety in perspectives toward the country state, as opposed to privileging a specific subset of those mentalities.

2. For perusers new to LCA, it is fundamental to note that the technique distinguishes classes dependent completely upon measurable standards, with practically no ramifications that individuals from the class so characterized address a social class or "class-for-itself."

3. Attitudinal overview information license one to make derivations about fundamental schemata yet mightn't in themselves at any point uncover such schemata. Indeed, even a moderately complete overview like GSS doesn't contain things that touch on each component of space; and the significance of a straight-out reaction might fluctuate among respondents. Strategies like LCA that quest for interpretable examples (and that can distinguish heterogeneous examples) can't dispense with the tradeoff between the extravagance of an interview or ethnographic information and the generalizability that overview information makes conceivable; however they push the tradeoff wilderness outward, allowing the investigator to approach schemata more intently than would some way or another be conceivable.

4. Although measurably desirable over elective determinations (both as an issue of general practice and model fit in our

examination), the consideration of covariates in the essential LCA model can influence the reaction probabilities of pointers by dormant class. To decide the degree to which this was the situation in our information, we demonstrated the connection between the patriotism pointers and dormant classes with and without covariates. The outcomes, accessible upon demand, didn't uncover any considerably significant contrasts. Of the 92 pairwise correlations of pointer implies across comparing classes, none were measurably critical.

5. The assessment of enormous quantities of boundaries in LCA models is computationally concentrated and may bring about model non-combination, so examiners utilize the size of the bivariate residuals to choose sets of factors for which the presumption of neighborhood autonomy can be loose. In our examinations, the accompanying sets of factors were allowed

to covary: pride in expressions and writing and pride in sports; pride in worldwide political impact and pride in majority rules government; pride in financial accomplishments and pride in worldwide political impact; pride in expressions and writing and pride in science and innovation; pride in America's set of experiences and pride in fair and equivalent treatment of all gatherings; understanding that America is superior to most nations and that it would be better on the off chance that more individuals were like Americans; communicating in English and being a resident as participation standards; being brought into the world in the US and living in the US for a large portion of one's life as enrollment measures; being brought into the world external the US and favoring U.S. citizenship to citizenship elsewhere, and being unequivocally strict and having confidence in Christianity as participation standard. LCA models with and without neighborhood conditions delivered meaningfully comparative outcomes.

6. To decide if our selection of pointers impacted the LCA results, we reran the models while progressively barring every individual marker. The substance of the classes yielded by the diminished models was predictable with the full model highlighting every one of the 23 pointers. Consequences of these heartiness checks are accessible upon demand. We thank a commentator for this idea.

7. We know about the dangerous implications of the expression "America," however we use it in our depiction of the information to mirror the genuine phrasing of the GSS patriotism things.

9. Much of the writing sees confidence in the significance of English as a type of ethnocultural patriotism (Citrin, Reingold, Walters, and Green 1990). In any case, as

Brubaker (2004:139) calls attention to, one can likewise describe strategies advancing a typical language as "emphatically municipal, that is to say, as irreplaceable for the advancement of conservative citizenship."

10. Respondents who communicated pride in parts of American history or establishments were most likely deciphering the inquiries likewise, however, the individuals who kept their pride might contrast extraordinarily in their reasons: for instance, individuals might need pride in the country's government-managed retirement framework since it is excessively liberal, excessively parsimonious, or excessively administrative; they might need pride in reasonableness and correspondence since they accept there is close to nothing or a lot of each, and they might need pride in America's worldwide impact since they feel the US has employed it too blunderingly or too specific.

11. Because the thing inquired as to whether individuals overall ought to help their nation when it is off-base, and not on the off chance that Americans ought to do as such, it is conceivable that a few respondents who differ accept that Americans ought to help their nation right or wrong, however, are not ready to hold residents of different nations to that equivalent norm.

12. Our class portrayals depend fundamentally on the extent of each sociodemographic classification that has a place with each class. however, we likewise cause intermittent notice of the extent of each class that has a place with each sociodemographic classification (tP-values for contrasts in model boundaries across classes are created by the fundamental LCA model with sociodemographic covariates utilizing Wald chi-squared tests (Vermunt and Magidson 2005).

13. Gender is just an imperceptibly measurably critical indicator of class enrollment, as represented by a p-worth of .061 in Table 2. Albeit strictly perceptive respondents seem, by all accounts, to be to some degree overrepresented among the enthusiastic patriots, the connection between legalism and class participation isn't measurably critical; the equivalent is valid for the geographic district.

14. Dividing the classes into progressively more modest subgroups, for example, Majority rule enthusiastic patriots who are non-white, raises the gamble of drawing derivations in light of little example sizes. Such discoveries ought to along these lines be seen as interesting as opposed to indisputable. This issue is just significant, be that as it may, in a couple of our between-class examinations and doesn't influence our general portrayal of the classes.

15. This finding recommends one potential instrument driving individuals to have a manageable distance toward America: their contending distinguishing proof with another country. Without a doubt, when non-residents are eliminated from the example, unfamiliar conceived respondents are no longer overrepresented among the separated. Citizenship status doesn't be that as it may, significantly influence the dissemination of unfamiliar conceived respondents across different classes or the appropriation of race by class. Moreover, because non-residents and unfamiliar conceived residents represent just 15% of the separated, distinguishing proof with different nations can't be deciphered as the essential driver of separation.

16. The investigation of citizenship and foreigner status among separated respondents depends on the modular class task in light of back probabilities produced by the LCA model (Bolck et al. 2004).

17. The overrepresentation of Hispanic respondents in this class may be part of the way reflect GSS examining rehearses. Preceding 2006, the GSS didn't direct meetings in Spanish, in this manner barring non-English-speaking Latino foreigners. The last option contrast extraordinarily with English-speaking Latinos both in sociodemographic attributes and perspectives (Smith 2007).

18. We additionally thought about the attitudinal profiles of leftists and conservatives inside each class to confirm that the classes were not concealing fundamental reaction heterogeneity by the party. The outcomes (accessible upon demand) didn't uncover significant contrasts in light of party in the attitudinal organization of the four classes.

19. Given the high financial status and territorial appropriation of creedal

conservatives, it would be sensible to anticipate that a significant number of them should work in science, innovation, and the callings and, generally speaking, to have moved to the US in a quest for word related open doors.

Extra examinations (results accessible upon demand) confirmed this instinct: among creedal conservatives, there is an overrepresentation of respondents utilized in designing, innovation, broadcasting, distributing, money, medication, and advanced education. Every one of the unfamiliar conceived conservatives contained in the general example has a place with the creedal patriot class, and they hail excessively from China, India, and Italy. There is an overrepresentation of Jewish and Hindu respondents, as well as respondents who list "other" as their religion.

20. To investigate this speculation further, we took advantage of three life fulfillment measures in the 2004 GSS, every one of which exploration has been viewed as an indicator of psychological well-being and every one of which (in comparative structure) has been a part of the mental prosperity scale utilized by numerous understudies of psychological well-being (Ryff and Keyes 1995). On the off chance that our instinct is right, the ardents ought to score higher on these actions than do the restrictives, and the creedal ought to score higher than the separated.

Without a doubt (results accessible upon demand), this is the very thing that we find: creedal patriots were more hopeful, self-assured, and trusting than were then separated, and enthusiastic patriots scored reliably higher on these three factors than did prohibitive patriots. Albeit these outcomes are not even close to dispositive, they recommend that examination of the connection between perspectives on the country and psychological well-being might be useful.

21. That prohibitive patriotism was more predominant than creedal patriotism in our example is additionally in conflict with research in the Tocquevillian custom that partners creedalism with the actual center of American public personality (e.g., Burnham 1982; Huntington 1981).

22. We would have gotten a kick out of the chance to inspect the connection between patriotism and political belief system — and party distinguishing proof — as well as the GSS variable that taps liberal-moderate self-ID was excluded from similar polling form as the public personality things.

23. The 2012 overview was controlled as a component of an examination project supported by the U.S. Marine Corps, on which the principal creator worked in a

warning limit. The respondents were haphazardly drawn from GfK's KnowledgePanel, a broadly delegate test at first distinguished through a blend of irregular digit dialing and address-based inspecting techniques.

24. The end that the more significant level of enthusiastic patriotism in 2004 is connected with the post-9/11 political environment is additionally upheld by our examinations of yearly Gallup information on trust in the military, Congress, and the administration (results accessible upon demand), which recommend that public help for state establishments expanded pointedly in late 2001 and remained moderately stable until somewhere around 2004.
Note additionally that the overall dependability of enthusiastic patriotism somewhere in the range between 2004 and 2012 happened even with the generational substitution of a few more established Americans, who were probably going to be

relegated to the impassioned classification, by more youthful Recent college grads (brought into the world somewhere in the range of 1987 and 1996 and in this manner not addressed in our 2004 information), who are significantly lower in both self-revealed positive energy and legalism than are more established companions (Seat Exploration Center 2014).

25. It is essential to take note that the prohibitive class incorporates an enormous portion of African American respondents, a voting demographic that has generally dismissed Donald Trump's nomination (to a great extent as a result of its mind-boggling distinguishing proof with the Progressive faction, yet additionally because of Trump's unmistakably racial governmental issues). The concurrence of African Americans and moderate whites in a similar class is a valuable wake-up call that various gatherings might buy into comparative thoughts for various reasons and with

various ramifications for political ways of
behaving.